MY GOLDEN NUGGETS

Life changing DEVOTIONS & meditations

CHAPLAIN RONNIE C. KING
CAPTAIN, UNITED STATES NAVY

LATTE COMMUNICATIONS Brothers

My Golden Nuggets
Life-Changing Devotions and Meditations
Copyright © 2011 by Ronnie C. King

For bookings or more information, please contact;
Curtis King, executiveoffice@tbaal.org

Published by:
Latte Brothers Communications Press
1030 E. Hwy. 377, Suite 110 Box 184
Granbury, TX 76048
www.LatteBros.com

Cover Design by Wicks Designs Inc.
www.WicksDesigns.com

ISBN - 978-0-9834869-2-3

Printed in the United States of America.

DEDICATION

This book is dedicated to the memory of my late father Jonah King, eldest brother Elmer K. King, and my grandparents James and L.A. McGhee, from whom I drew great strength and wisdom. This book also is dedicated to my mother Elizabeth McGhee King, my son Nigell King, brother Vernon King, and to all those individuals who believed in me enough to request my Thoughts for the Day. I especially dedicate this book to my brother Curtis King, a great mentor whose examples have inspired me to strive for higher heights, stay focused upon my calling and to never settle for less when I can have more. This book has become a reality because of his encouragement, vision, leadership and guidance.

ABOUT THE AUTHOR

Chaplain Ronnie C. King,
Captain, United States Navy

"Perseveres through the toughest challenges and inspires others."

U.S. Navy Captain Ronnie C. King has earned the highest rating the Navy offers, and he has earned it for several years.

The honor reads: "Perseveres through the toughest challenges and inspires others."

No finer words could be used to describe the services Captain King provides for thousands of U.S. Navy, Marine Corps and Coast Guard personnel, their families, civilians, and his country.

His heart felt approach has addressed both the emotional and spiritual needs of individuals as well as groups and organizations. In an ecumenical manner, he has provided guidance and support in the areas of family crises, suicide prevention, relationship problems, deployment issues and combat operational stress, providing words that convey concern, compassion and insight in each instance. Because of his unselfish nature, he is able to effectively be present in situations where others might hesitate to venture.

Captain King is well-respected by the men and women he has served, praised for his extraordinary work ethics by his commanders, trusted as a leader by those who have served under his command, and recognized for his exceptional skills by fellow officers and chaplains.

From humble beginnings and turbulent times in Coldwater, Mississippi, Captain King graduated from Coldwater High School. With strong persuasion, sincere encouragement and loving support from his mother, Elizabeth McGhee King, he completed his undergraduate degree in Political Science from Ole Miss, The University of Mississippi. He went on to earn a Masters of Theology from The Perkins School of Theology at Southern Methodist University in Dallas, Texas. Captain King holds also a Masters of Science degree in National Security Strategy from the National Defense University in Washington, D.C.

Military Service
Captain King has been stationed at Camp Lejeune, NC; Newport, RI; Parris Island, SC; San Diego, CA; Portsmouth, VA; and Kaneohe Bay, HI. He has served in Iraq, South and Central America, Haiti and Africa. He deployed aboard the USS RALEIGH (LPD-1) during the Persian Gulf Crisis and served as command chaplain aboard the USS McKEE. He later deployed as the group chaplain during Operation Iraqi Freedom.

Promotions
1984 - Lieutenant Junior Grade
1985 - Lieutenant
1992 - Lieutenant Commander
1998 - Commander
2003 - Captain

Accomplishments
Some of his many accomplishments and recognitions:

• delivered the eulogy for Captain Fredrick C. Branch, the first African American officer in the United States Marine Corps.

• initiated strategic placement of chaplains throughout Anbar and Ninewa providences in Iraq to best serve the needs of military personnel and their families.

• hosted the largest 2nd MAW Ecumenical Prayer Breakfast in station history with over 100 military and community leaders from multiple faiths in attendance.

• developed and initiated a system for tracking, analyzing, and recording of the delivery of ministerial programs to over 30,000 Marines, Sailors, family members and civilians.

• instituted and managed the first-ever family readiness meeting for over ninety 2d MAW Key Volunteers, which set the standard for all future meetings.

• received the Defense Meritorious Service Medal for outstanding performance as the CJTF HOA Command Chaplain for his work in establishing exceptional rapport with regional governmental and non-governmental agencies.

• revived a struggling Religious Ministry Program and turned it into the Mid-Atlantic Region's best in its 60-year-history of the air station.

• served as Director of Religious Affairs for international relations with Religious Leaders in Comoros, Seychelle Islands, Uganda, and Tanzania. Speaker at the Eid Al Fitr dinner for Muslim and other members of Parliament hosted by Ambassador Cesar Cabrera in the Republic of Mauritius.

• provided the foundation for a critical meeting with Religious Leaders of Tanzania; the first such meetings in several years.

• implemented plans that provided 24-hour chaplain access to over 15,000 Sailors, dependents and family members at NASB, WING FIVE and all tenant commands.

• developed and implemented a 30-60-90-120 Days plan for Marines and Sailors to decompress and reintegrate back into family and society after deployment.

• contributed to the Combined Task Force Haiti, working with officers and enlisted personnel from the U.S., France, Canada, and Chile.

• trained and deployed six Religious Ministries Teams to Afghanistan, Kuwait, and Iraqi in support of the War on Terrorism in support of Navy and Marine personnel.

CONTENTS

ACKNOWLEDGMENTS

There are so many people to thank and acknowledge for making this book possible. If I inadvertently omit someone, please know that it is not by choice. So I want to thank all of you in advance for your encouragement, words of wisdom, and contributions. Thank you Kelly Dippold, my sister and friend in Christ, who approached me during my tour of duty at 2d Marine Aircraft Wing, Cherry Point, North Carolina about starting a "thought for the day" to encourage others.

Thanks to Anita Aker for making and keeping copies of devotionals and for researching various links and websites to glean my past accomplishments. You'll always hold a special place in my heart!

Thank you Sharon Egiebor and the Egiebor Expressions team, my editors who labored with the material presented to them and allowed God to guide the organization of the meditations in a systematic way. I would like to give a special thanks to Myyon Hardeman, who typed the initial draft to ensure the editor could read the manuscript.

Thanks to Barry Jenkins, my publisher who provided invaluable insights and guidance during the entire process. Barry worked tirelessly to make sure that my book would be a first-class product.

Thanks to Chadwicks Design for designing the cover. His company has to be one of the best in the business! Thanks my brother for your keen insight and talented designer's eye. Your cover design is off the charts!

And finally, thanks to my brother, mentor and motivator, Curtis King. Had it not been for Curtis, this book would never have come to fruition. His unwavering support and mentorship, especially during the low moments of my life when this process seems to have been extremely daunting, is monumental.

Thanks!

Ronnie

INTRODUCTION

The Thoughts and Meditations for the Day began as a way to encourage myself and to counsel my parishioners -- the men and women I serve as Navy chaplain. Initially, it was a small list, averaging between 20 and 30 people. In time, family, friends, colleagues, comrades and strangers asked to be included.

Many people said they found comfort in these thoughts and felt the need to pass them on to others. The request list kept growing and people from around the world asked me to add their names to the email list. Some wrote saying they use my Thoughts for their daily morning devotions and meditations. In fact, the title originated from a reader's comments. "Sir, I love and enjoy reading your Thoughts for the Day. I call them my little golden nuggets," she wrote.

You will notice that the scriptures are pulled from several versions of the bible, ranging from the New Living Translation to the Howland Christian Standard Bible to the New International Version, etc. In the process of writing, I picked up whatever version was available to me at the time I felt the inspiration from the Holy Spirit. There were times when God spoke to me while I was personally under attack from others, my parishioners (as I called them) were facing challenges and there were times when I was flying through the hostile and dangerous skies of Iraq. Over a period of time, I realized that I had written hundreds of daily thoughts from almost every corner of America and the world.

Finally, the publishing of this book of meditations were conceived around my mother's kitchen table. My older brother, Curtis, said that I should put all of my thoughts in a book for others to read and perhaps use as their daily devotions and meditations. By the way, Curtis was a recipient of the daily meditations as well. So, I listened to Curtis with some reservation and hesitation, but in the end the book idea took flight with the thoughts and meditations included in these pages.

As difficult as some of these thoughts were to write at the time, I now find great joy in sharing them. I pray that you will be blessed and encouraged by the Spirit of God as you read each devotion and meditation.

Chaplain Ronnie C. King

MY GOLDEN NUGGETS

Life changing DEVOTIONS & meditations

CHAPLAIN RONNIE C. KING
CAPTAIN, UNITED STATES NAVY

Senator Barack Obama (D-ILL), left, receives a special prayer written for him by
Chaplain Ronnie C. King, right, while LTJG Romero, center looks on during the Senator's visit to
Djibouti, Africa in September 2006.

A SPECIAL PRAYER WRITTEN FOR SENATOR BARACK OBAMA

In September 2006, while serving duty in Djibouti, Africa, Illinois Senator Barack Obama (D), now President of the United States, was visiting us at Camp Lemonier. I had the wonderful opportunity of playing basketball with Senator Obama. When the game was over, Senator Obama chatted with some of us. He and I teased each other about our basketball shortcomings. The senator said, "Chaplain, I hope you are a better chaplain than you are a basketball player." I chuckled and replied, "Senator, I may not be a good basketball player, but I can pray." He responded, "Well, pray for me, Chaplain." We departed.

The next day, I saw Senator Obama again and I said, "Senator, you asked me to pray for you so I went home last night and wrote you a prayer." "You did?" He replied. "Would you share it with me?" I told him I would be honored to do so. The prayer I wrote and shared with then Senator Obama is, I believe, appropriate to share with the readers of this book of thoughts and meditations.

Our gracious God, before whom all secrets are known and all hearts are disclosed, we ask your blessings upon this thy servant, Senator Barack Obama, whom we bless in your name.

We pray that you continue to be with him as he walks up and down the halls and corridors of Congress and Capitol Hill.

We ask your guidance for him as he attends meetings, speaks on the floor of Congress, meets with other senators, representatives, presidents, ambassadors, heads of states, dignitaries, and everyone with whom he comes in contact.

We pray that when he is faced with tough choices, difficult decisions, and unpopular political issues, that you will give him the wisdom of Solomon, the courage of Joshua, the leadership of Moses and the strength of David.

We ask, Lord, that you always be his light and his salvation ... that you always defeat his enemies, silence his critics and expose those who would come against him.

Finally, Lord, we pray the prayer over Senator Obama that Moses prayed over your people:

"The Lord bless thee and keep thee,
The Lord make his face to shine upon thee and be gracious to thee,
The Lord lift up his countenance upon thee and give thee peace."

Amen.

By Chaplain Ronnie C. King, Navy Captain

DEVOTIONALS

"Why am I at this particular place?"

Purpose

Scripture: *"Don't think for a moment that you will escape there in the palace when all other Jews are killed. If you keep quiet at a time like this, deliverance for the Jews will arise from some other place, but you and your relatives will die. What's more, who can say but that you have been elevated to the palace for just such a time as this?"*

(Esther 4:3-13 NLT)

DEVOTIONAL

Have you ever wondered why you are where you are now? Has the question ever crossed your mind, "Why am I at this particular place, working with these particular people, having to endure this particular issue or problem?" Well, if you are like me, I have asked those and many other questions. But the answer keeps coming back the same, "Who can say but that you have been elevated for such a time as this?" Whether we realize it or not, God places each of us where He wants us, and we are there to serve his purpose.

Esther had to be reminded by her uncle (Mordecai) that she had been elevated to the rank of queen, not for her own glory, but for the glory of God. God knew that Haman would devise an evil plan to kill all the Jews, so He placed Esther in the right place, at the right place, at the right time, to do the right thing—to speak to her husband (the king) on behalf of her people.

God knows where you and I are. He knows where we are working. He knows what we are faced with. The next time you are tempted to say "Why me?" just remember, "Who can say but that you have been elevated to the palace for just such a time as this?"

God bless!

Chaplain King takes a class trip with the National War College, based in Washington, D.C.

No Worries

Scripture: *"And we know that all things work together for good to them that love God, to them who are the called according to his purpose."*

(Romans 8:28 KJV)

DEVOTIONAL

Let's think about this scripture. Let me restate what it says: "And we know that all things work together for the good to them that love God, to them who are the called according to his purpose." If we reflect upon the words stated, we realize that whatever happens in our lives, if we "love" God, it works for our "good." Everything? Yes, everything works for our good, even the bad things that occur occasionally. Yes, even the hardship that I have to endure occasionally. When God says "all things," He means exactly that—all things!

Webster defines "all" as follows: "The whole of," "beyond all doubt," "entirely," "completely." Therefore, my (your) life is completely/entirely/beyond all doubt, controlled by God who is able to keep you and to sustain you. As you go throughout the day, rejoice in the fact that whatever comes your way, God is in control completely and He will work it out "for your good." Take advantage of this truth and be "worry free" for today! Don't worry about tomorrow, because the same God who controls your today will control your tomorrow!

God bless!

Chaplain King receives his Masters of Science degree in National Security Strategy from the National Defense University, based in Washington, D.C.

Pridefulness

Scripture: *"Pride goes before destruction, and haughtiness before a fall."*

(Proverbs 16:18 NLT)

DEVOTIONAL

Pride is a deadly disease that will eat away at the core of your/ my inner being. It can creep upon you without warning, without notice, and without a heads up. We have to guard ourselves through constant prayer to ensure that this deadly disease does not become a part of our daily or normal living. Equally deadly is arrogance and this, too, will derail you/me in such a way that it may take years to recover! A friend of mine sent me a "Daily Motivator" that beautifully states what both pride and arrogance are all about. The adapted version is below.

Arrogance or Pride is the worst kind of loneliness because it is entirely self-imposed. If you become impressed with your own importance, everyone else ceases to be impressed at all. The worst kind of ignorance is to think you know it all, for that is an ignorance into which you sink more deeply as each moment passes. Those who are most genuinely admired are those who have no need to be admired. The real experts are those who spend their time listening and learning rather than boasting and preening. Humility is a virtue that will carry you far. When you are free from the rushing demands of ego, there is so very much more you can accomplish. Let go of the need to be better than others and you'll free yourself to reach magnificent heights of success and fulfillment.

And all the people said, "Amen."

God bless!

Chaplain King standing on the bridge over the Nile River during a trip to Lira, Uganda,
December 6-8, 2006.

Wagging Tongues

Scripture*: "The heart of the righteous weighs its answers, but the mouth of the wicked gushes evil."*

(Proverbs 15:28 NLT)

DEVOTIONAL

The tongue can be a deadly weapon! I remember growing up hearing the saying, "Sticks and stones may break my bones, but words can never hurt me." Well, it doesn't take long to realize that this "old saying" is BADLY wrong. Words in fact *can* and *do* hurt us, and in many instances we have used words to do just that: *to hurt others*. Some will take the position that what was said needed to be said, and if it hurt the person, then so be it. But is that the godly and/or righteous way of doing things? Or should we (as Proverbs says) weigh our answers and/or responses? Many times I have heard people say, "WWJD" (What would Jesus do?) but in their responses to others, they do exactly the opposite of what Jesus would do.

My challenge to each of us today is to think about or "weigh" our answers to others today. Let us think before we speak and ask God to help us to control our tongues!

God bless!

"If God called you home right now, where would you go?"

Timing

Scripture: *"There is a time for everything, a season for every activity under heaven."*

(Ecclesiastes 3:1 NLT)

DEVOTIONAL

I attended a memorial service yesterday. On my way back from the service, I thought deeply about the fact that none of us know exactly when the trumpet will sound and we will be called home. During the ride back on our C-130, the thought crossed my mind that this could be my last ride and I began to reflect (briefly) about my life. I asked myself several questions that I'd like to challenge you to ask as well.

If God called you home right now, where would you go?

Have you lived your life in such a way that God is pleased with you?

What will the minister/preacher/chaplain say about you when your time has come to close your eyes in death?

Let me apologize if I sound a bit morbid to you—I don't mean to do so. However, I think these are important questions that we all need to answer! Why? The writer of Ecclesiastes says, "There is a time for everything, a season for every activity under heaven. A time to be born and a time to die." There are those who live their lives as if they have eternity when in fact they only have "today."

My challenge to each of us is to ensure that we can answer the above questions, to live each day to its fullest for the Lord and not for self, to be prepared to hear the trumpet of the Lord sound when He orders his angel to blow it.

Be blessed. Be prayerful. Be faithful.

God bless!

Chaplain King prepares for class at the National War College.

The Body of Christ

Scripture: *"The human body has many parts, but the many parts make up only one body."*

(I Corinthians 12:12 NLT)

DEVOTIONAL

Have you ever thought about the fact that you and I are only "one part" of the "one body?" If you have, then think for a moment about how exactly do you/I affect the overall body. Does my one body part bring praise to the overall body or do I bring harm to the overall body? Why would I /you do something that would hurt my arm, my eye, my leg, and so forth? Recently I had shoulder surgery and believe me, when I go to physical therapy and they work my shoulder, it hurts my whole body. In other words, what I do to one part of my body affects the other parts. My actions and yours, as one body part, affect the whole body of Christ.

The next time we are tempted to be harsh, mean, or hurtful to another person, stop and think. He/she is a part of your/my body and what you and I do to someone else, we are also doing to ourselves. Think about it!

God bless!

"Are my prayers hindered?"

Unforgiveness

Scripture: *"And forgive us our sins, just as we have forgiven those who have sinned against us."*

(Matthew 6:12 NLT)

DEVOTIONAL

Now, here is something to really ponder! Are my prayers hindered because of my inability or refusal to forgive? Hum! Got your attention? I hope so, because it is crucial that we understand the nature and depth of what Christ is saying when He says, "Forgive us our sins [or trespasses] as we forgive those who sin [or trespass] against us." We must understand that God's decision to forgive us is contingent upon our being willing to forgive others. There are those of us who've been walking around for days, weeks, months, and years with our prayers unanswered because we have an unforgiving spirit. I know some are saying, "Well he/she got what he/she deserved" or "he/she needs to be held accountable," and both statements could possibly be true. But here's the deal. When holding one accountable, it should be done in a spirit of love and not malicious false piety. Is it difficult to forgive someone who has hurt you, betrayed you, backstabbed you, and done a host of other things to you? Yes, but it is necessary.

Forgiveness sets us free from the pain of holding on to past and present hurts; forgiveness delivers us from the bondage of anger, resentment, confusion, and depression. Search your heart today—be honest—and take that unforgiving spirit to the Lord. He is waiting and He wants to set you free!

God bless!

"Have you ever heard Him?"

Intimacy

Scripture: *"Toward evening they heard the Lord God walking about in the garden."*

(Genesis 3:8 NLT)

DEVOTIONAL

When is the last time you heard the Lord God "walking in the garden" to have a conversation with you? Have you ever heard Him? When is the last time you have taken a morning, noon, or evening stroll, during which you heard the voice of God coming toward you? Or have you been so busy with work, watching TV, caught up in self, or doing a host of other things that you just haven't slowed down long enough to hear the voice of the Lord?

I know—this sounds a bit strange (hearing the voice of God)—but that is exactly what happened to Adam and Eve. They were in God's garden, and they heard God's footsteps (if you will) walking toward them. For the first time, they ran away from God instead of running toward God. Up to this point, Adam and Eve's relationship with God had been one of praise and joy, but now they found themselves "hiding" and "running" away from the one with whom they had enjoyed talking daily.

Another question to ask yourself is, "Have you ever found yourself running from God?" I have and I didn't like the feeling. I didn't like the feeling because I missed the talks! I didn't like the feeling because I missed the daily conversation. I didn't like the feeling because I was separated from the very one who brought me total joy and happiness: God! Why was I running? Like Adam and Eve, I had disobeyed God. How did I rectify the situation? I stopped running and I stopped hiding. Instead of continuing to run and hide from God, I ran toward God and (as Adam and Eve did) confessed my disobediences. Guess what? He clothed me in his righteousness of grace, mercy, love, and forgiveness! Wow! Pretty cool, huh? To know that when you/I disobey God we can run to Him (not away from Him) and receive his forgiveness, grace, love, and mercy! He holds us accountable, yes, but as David said, "Even in his anger, He (God) is merciful!"

Praise the Lord! Remember to run toward God, not away from Him! If you want some help with this, call me!

God bless!

Lies

Scripture: *"You won't die."*

(Genesis 3:4 NLT)

DEVOTIONAL

"Y ou won't die."
   "Really?"
"Of course not. God is lying. Go ahead and eat from the tree that God has marked off limits. It won't hurt a thing!"

Yesterday, I asked you when you had last heard the voice of God talking to you. Today, I'm asking when you last heard that other person (okay, the devil) talking to you. Was it a few minutes ago? Maybe, but even if it was not a few minutes ago, just wait. He will definitely contact you to have a conversation. And, I can promise you one thing: he will definitely contradict everything that God tells you. I guarantee it! He will counter-punch, restate and/or rephrase God's words (or comments) to you and try his very best to get you to doubt everything that God has promised.

Please remember this, if there is a liar (when it comes to what God says and what the devil says), the liar is always going to be the devil. Remember this, too. The devil has one thing in mind for you: "to kill, steal and to destroy." He wants to destroy you totally, steal your joy and happiness, and kill your relationships with God and others. If you want this to happen (for him to kill, steal, and destroy you), then continue to listen to him contradict what God is saying to you. If you want to prevent this from happening, then don't listen to him when he says, "It is okay to eat. You won't die." Be certain that, if God says, "Don't eat for the day in which you do, you shall surely die," He means exactly that!

Listen only to the voice of God!

God bless!

Chaplain King visiting a baby orphanage in Lira, Uganda.

Freedom

Scripture: *"The Lord protects the upright but destroys the wicked."*

(Proverbs 10:29 NLT)

DEVOTIONAL

One of my greatest challenges is to trust the Lord to handle everything for me or in my life, especially when it comes to dealing with difficult people. I am a "fix it" type of guy and my "fix it" attitude causes me much frustration at times. What I have discovered is that I can alleviate this frustration, if (and when) I keep in mind that "the battle is not mine but it is the Lord's." Man (or woman), what a relief! When I finally get it through my thick skull that "The Lord protects the upright but destroys the wicked," I stop having sleepless and restless nights (or days). When I sit back ... take a deep breath ... PRAY... and meditate on the word or words of God, I can release that "fix it" attitude and let God protect me as He promised to do. I don't know about you, but that's what I call "freedom."

Remember on this blessed day that you are His and He spoke these sacred words to you and over you: "The Lord protects the upright but destroys the wicked."

God bless!

Chaplain King visits a refugee camp in Uganda.

Majesty

Scripture*:* *"He spreads out the northern [skies] over empty space; He suspends the earth over nothing."*

(Job 26:6-14 NIV)

DEVOTIONAL

I tell you my friend, sometimes God's word just gives me goose bumps. (Do you ever experience that?) Reading Job 26:6-14 makes for one of those goose bumps time. I find myself emotional and tearful as I read the awesome testimony that Job gives about the power of God. Job describes a vivid picture of God's mighty power, and he concludes in verse 14 by saying, "these are some of the minor things He does, merely a whisper of His power." Just listen (if you will) to how mighty is our God:

> Death is naked before God;
> Destruction lies uncovered.
> He spreads out the northern skies over empty space;
> *(Wow, do you feel them yet? My words!)*
> He suspends the earth over nothing.
> He wraps up the waters in His clouds,
> Yet the clouds do not burst under their weight.
> He covers the face of the full moon,
> Spreading His clouds over it.
> He marks out the horizon on the face of the water
> For a boundary between light and darkness.
> The pillars of the heavens quake, at His rebuke.
> By His power He churned up the sea;

By His wisdom He cut Rahab to pieces;
By His breath the skies became fair;
His hand pierced the sliding serpent.

And these are some of the minor things He does, merely a whisper of his power.

I don't know about you, but I'm so thankful that I serve a God who is powerful and MORE.

And all the people said, "Amen."

God bless!

Change

Scripture: *"The Lord blessed the latter part of Job's life more than the first."*

(Job 42:12 NIV)

DEVOTIONAL

"It ain't over until the fat lady (or fat man) sings." How many times have we heard that saying when it comes to a baseball, basketball, or football game when our team is behind? We hold out for hope, a prayer, or a miracle that our team will catch up, come from behind, and win the game. Yet, when it comes to our own lives we seem to write God off, give up hope, and give in to the particular situation with which we are confronted. Too often we focus (too much) on our problems rather than on our problem solver. If Job had listened to his friends, and yes, even to his wife, he would have given up, cursed God, and died.

Whether Job's wife and friends were suggesting suicide or not I don't know, but their suggestion seemed a bit premature since God had not written the final chapter of Job's life. Just think for a moment, what if Job had listened to his wife and friends? What if Job had looked at his current situation and given up? What if Job had not spoken the words, "I will wait until my change comes"? Had he done that, we would not be able to read the encouraging words of Job 42:12: "The Lord blessed the latter part of Job's life more than the first." Had Job accepted the advice of his wife and friends, he would have missed a POWERFUL blessing because he listened to the voices of others. For Job, it wasn't a question of *if* his change was going to come, but *when* his change was going to come. He knew that it was going to come; there was no doubt!

My friends, when trials and tribulations come our way (and they will), we should not listen to the skeptics and critics. Doubters should NEVER determine our faith. Even when no one agrees with you, but God has spoken to you, stand fast. Hold on to what God has said and remember that what God did for Job, He will do for you also. "The Lord blessed the latter part of Job's life more than the first."

God bless!

Obedience

Scripture: *"Come, I will send you to Pharaoh that you may bring My people, the children of Israel, out of Egypt."*

(Exodus 3:10 ESV)

DEVOTIONAL

God does not always call us to do easy things! Many times He will call us to do what appears to be impossible, or if not impossible, at least very challenging. I'm sure it was not easy for Moses to go before a powerful king and say to him, "The God of Abraham, Isaac and Jacob told me to tell you to let My people go." I can only imagine the look that Pharaoh gave Moses when he uttered those words. In this day and time, Pharaoh's response would probably be, "Yeah. Right!" Scary thing for Moses to do? I'm sure it was! A fearful thing for Moses to do? I'm sure it was! A necessary thing for Moses to do? Definitely! It was necessary because God had ordered him to do it.

Moses could have refused the orders and gone UA (unauthorized absence), but he would have been running for the rest of his life. Also, he would not have been at peace, because he would have been out of the will of God. So what did Moses do? He said, "Yes, Lord." Then God told him these awesome words, "I will be with you."

My brothers and sisters, when God calls us to do something, He does several things: (1) He goes with us; (2) He equips us for the journey and/or task that He has called us to do; (3) He gives us the tools to accomplish the job. Think about it. God gave Moses a shepherd's staff!

Seems simple to the human mind, but to the faithful that shepherd's staff turned into a serpent at Moses' command. To the faithful that shepherd's staff swallowed up Pharaoh's snakes. To the faithful that shepherd's staff turned water into blood. The point is, when God calls you to do a job, the job may be tough, but He will equip you with his "shepherd's staff."

Go in peace. Go in faith. Go in the blessed assurance that God has assured you (as He did Moses) that "I will be with you."

God bless!

No Excuses

Scripture: *"But Moses said to the Lord, 'Oh, my Lord, I am not eloquent, either in the past or since you have spoken to your servant, but I am slow of speech and of tongue.'"*

(Exodus 4:10 ESV)

DEVOTIONAL

Excuses, excuses, excuses. Moses attempted to give God several excuses as to why he should not go to Egypt to face Pharaoh. God's response to each excuse was "beautiful" as well as reassuring:

Moses' excuse: They will ask which god are you talking about? What is his name? What shall I tell them?

God's answer: Tell them that I Am the One Who Always Is. Just tell them I Am has sent me to you.

Moses' excuse: They won't believe me! They won't do what I tell them!

God's answer: Throw down your shepherd's staff. (It turned into a snake.) Now, pick it up by the tail. (It turned back into the shepherd's staff!) Now put your hands into your robe. (His hand turned snow white like leprosy.) Now, do it again. (The hand turned back to normal.)

Moses' excuse: I'm just not a good speaker.

God's answer: Who makes mouths? Who makes people so they can speak or not speak, hear or not hear, see or not see? Is it not I, the Lord? Now go and do as I have told you. I will help you speak well, and I will tell you what to say.

Do you get the picture? Moses offered God several excuses why he was not a good candidate to send to Egypt, but God countered with POWER. With each answer, God assured Moses that he, the Lord, was able to handle Pharaoh and anything else. With each answer, God showed Moses that the Lord had the power to accomplish the mission through Moses. It reminds me of the Apostle Paul's words, "I can do all things through Christ who give me strength."

You see, my friends, it's not about you or me. It's not about power. It's not about our eloquent speech. It's not about intelligence. It's not about us at all. IT IS ALL ABOUT GOD.

God bless!

The Art of "Keep"

Scripture: *"Ask, and it will be given to you; seek, and you will find; knock, and it will be opened to you. For everyone who asks receives, and the one who seeks finds, and to the one who knocks it will be opened."*

(Matthew 7: 7-8 ESV)

DEVOTIONAL

Man, this is good stuff! Read Matthew 7:7-8 again, but this time pause after each sentence and think about what Christ says. First, He says, "Keep asking." In other words, be persistent in your asking. "Keep searching"—don't give up because you don't receive what you are praying about the first, second, or third time. "Keep knocking"—when you come across what appears to be a closed door (or what actually is a closed door), Christ is saying, keep on knocking and the door will be opened to you. Too many times we give up on asking, seeking, searching, and knocking because things don't happen when we think they should. Too many times we put a time limit on God and try to make or force God to do things in our time and not in his time. Many times we are too impatient, and our impatience causes us to move out in a direction or to make a decision, only to regret our choices later. Develop the art of "keep" when it comes to your prayer life. Keep asking until God answers and He will! Keep searching until God directs your path and He will! Keep knocking until God opens the door that He wants you to go through and He will!

God bless!

Chaplain King holding baby during his trip to a refugee camp in Africa.

Perfect Peace

Scripture: *"You will keep in perfect peace all who trust in you, whose thoughts are fixed on you!"*

(Isaiah 26:3 NLT)

DEVOTIONAL

I have often thought about how to have constant and steady peace of mind. Have you? At times I listen to the news, read the newspaper, or just listen to people talk, and I ask the question, "How can one have peace of mind with so many things going on?" Even this past week with Hurricane Ike, rising gas prices, and the news of two major companies going belly-up, some will begin to worry about their IRAs, 401(k)s, and a host of other issues. So the question is, "How can we not worry about all these things?" Isaiah 26:3 gives us the key to not only having a worry free life, but (also) how not to focus on and become wrapped up, tied up, and tangled up in what is happening with the stock market and gas prices. Listen to what Isaiah says: "You [God] will keep in perfect peace all who trust in you, whose thoughts are fixed on you." Wow! Not only will God keep you in "peace," He will keep you in "PERFECT" peace. But here's the deal. In order to have this "perfect peace," one must first "trust in Him/God," and secondly, "fix your thoughts" on God. The word "fix" means "to make firm, stable or to fasten or attach firmly." Isaiah is saying that if we want to have peace of mind, then we must "make firm, or fasten our thoughts on God." In other words, we must "lock" our thoughts on God and his power and control! The more we fix, fasten, or lock our thoughts on God, the more we will have "peace of mind."

Try it. It works!

God bless!

Chaplain King visiting Otino-Waa in Lira, Uganda.

Commitment

Scripture: *"But even if He doesn't, we want to make it clear to you, Your Majesty, that we will never serve your gods or worship the gold statue you have set up."*

(Daniel 3:18 NLT)

DEVOTIONAL

"But even if He doesn't!" Now that's when you know you are serving God out of love and not for what He can do for you. When you're able to say with a pure heart and clean conscience, "even if He doesn't deliver me from the blazing furnace, I will not serve your gods or worship the gold statue," then you know your heart is in the right place. Can you say that? This is not a trick question, but it *is* a serious one! When you're faced with disappointment ... when you didn't receive that prayer request ... when you didn't get that promotion ... when you fasted and prayed but it didn't turn out the way you wanted ... are you still able to say, "But even if not, I will not bow to the 'golden statue' of depression, anger, resentment, etc.?"

You see my friends, Shadrach, Meshach, and Abednego had what I call a "But if not" relationship with God. They knew that God was able and capable of delivering them from the hands of Nebuchadnezzar and from the blazing furnace, but they didn't know whether or not He would. They knew He had the power to deliver, but the question remained whether or not He would. The issue for them, however, was not the power of God nor was it whether or not God would deliver them. The issue was their relationship with and commitment to God. They made the decision that they would rather die in a blazing furnace than to sacrifice their relationship with and commitment to God. To them their relationship with and their commitment to God meant more than life itself. Their relationship to God meant more than any prestige, money, promotion, job, ANYTHING. This was true commitment and true love!

Think about it!

God bless!

Quarrels

Scripture: *"For it has been reported to me ... that there is quarrels among you."*

(1 Corinthians 1:11 ESV)

DEVOTIONAL

"Can't we all just get along?" This phrase became very popular in 1991 when Rodney King spoke it during the Los Angeles riots. If you recall, he spoke these words after he had been beaten by police officers and in an attempt to bring peace and harmony to a very ugly situation in Los Angeles. I don't think the Apostle Paul was dealing with riots when he said to the Corinthian Christians, "Now I urge you in the name of our Lord Jesus Christ that you all say the same thing, that there be no divisions among you and that you be united with the same understanding and the same conviction." However, he was dealing with a situation that could destroy the church: quarrelling among the members. They were arguing over what I call silliness: whether one was baptized by Paul, Apollo, or Cephas. Sound ridiculous? It was, and Paul, in so many words, said so. But we can't be too hard on the Corinthian Christians, for we, too, get wrapped around the axle on many silly issues and destroy relationships over things that matter to us but don't matter to God. Many times we go as far as to stop speaking to a co-worker, friend, and (yes) family member over things that matter very little to God.

Here's a question, if something doesn't matter to God, then why should it matter so much to us? Why do we fight battles that are not ours to fight? Why do we destroy relationships that do not have to be destroyed? Why do we allow our pride and ego to cause us to do and say things that, deep down within, we know are not pleasing to God? Is it more important to be at peace with one another or to appease our pride and ego? As we go throughout the day today, let's strive to be at peace with one another, especially with that or those individual(s) who get on our last nerve!

God bless!

Praise

Scripture: *"I will thank you, Lord, with all my heart: I will tell of all the marvelous things you have done. I will be filled with joy because of you. I will sing praises to your name, O Most High."*

(Psalm 9: 1-2 NLT)

Devotional

D o you ever get the Monday morning blues? I do, and to be honest, I have them now. So I opened my Bible and decided to read the first page that it opened to—Psalm 9. When I read the psalm, my Monday morning blues left me immediately. (Try it.) Just reading the first two verses freed me from the blues because the psalmist starts off by "thanking the Lord." He says, "I will thank the Lord, with all my heart; I will tell of all the marvelous things you have done."

When I read that and thought about all the marvelous things that God has done for me, my Monday morning blues took a hike. I thought about the wonderful time I had at church on Sunday; I thought about the tasty shrimp curry that I made on Saturday (and it was good…smile); I thought about the nice bike ride that I went on Sunday afternoon; I thought about the many positive comments that I have received since God has blessed us to supply a "Thought for the Day;" I thought about the many blessings that God has blessed me with in spite of all the bad news that we have been hearing about this economy; I thought about the peaceful rest that He allowed me to have over the weekend. As I read and reflected upon the first two verses, I thought about SOOOOOO MANY things to be thankful for and guess what? My blues left me and I started smiling. Can't you see this BIG smile on my face? If not, I assure you it is there. Try it. Listen to the words. Let the words sink deep into your mind and spirit." I will thank you, Lord, with all my heart; I will tell of all the MARVELOUS things you have done. I will be FILLED with JOY because of you. I WILL SING PRAISES TO YOUR NAME."

God bless!

Distinction

Scripture: *"I will make a clear distinction between your people and My people."*

(Exodus 8:23 NLT)

DEVOTIONAL

God is awesome! Now, I know you have heard me say that many times, but it's true. He really is awesome. Here's what I mean: when God brought about the ten plagues upon the Egyptian people, none of them affected the children of Israel. When the Egyptians' houses were swarming with flies, the children of God were not affected at all. When the livestock of the Egyptian people were dying, not a one died that belonged to the children of God. When darkness fell upon the Egyptian people, there was light in the land where God's people lived. God made a "clear distinction" between his people and the Egyptians.

Why do I say that He is awesome? It's because He is still making a "clear distinction" between those who are His people and those who are not today. There are those who can't see the distinction because they are blinded by their own disbelief! There are those that can't see the distinction because they are not receiving the things that they think they should, so they become hardened. There are those who can't see the distinction because they are looking for God to handle things their way instead of allowing Him to handle things his way.

Yes, God is awesome! Yes, God is still saying, "I will make a clear distinction between your people and My people!" Yes, even in the midst of a trying and challenging time, there will be peace for God's people in the midst of chaos ... there will be light shining around God's people while others are in darkness ... and there will be security for God's people while others are insecure. Why? Because God is an awesome God and He makes a clear distinction in favor of his people!

Stay encouraged!

God bless!

Saintly Prayers

Scripture: *"For this reason I bow my knees before the Father from whom every family in heaven and on earth is named."*
(Ephesians 3:14-15 NIV)

DEVOTIONAL

Paul prayed a special prayer for the saints and believers in Christ at Ephesus. If you get a moment, read Ephesians 3:14-21 and you will be blessed by the prayer that he prayed for the saints and for us. He prayed that they be strengthened with power. He prayed that the Messiah dwell in their hearts. He prayed that they comprehend the depth of God's love. He prayed that they be filled with all the fullness of God. I'd like to pray a special prayer for you. Will you join me?

Lord, I join Paul in praying for my brothers and sisters who have joined me in this daily devotion. I am grateful for their comments, their encouragement, and their commitment to spend a few moments each day to think about the many blessings that you bless them with daily. Also, I am grateful for the encouragement they give me, which allows me to continue to stay committed to your word, your will and your ways. I ask that you keep them safe, that their time with family, friends and loved ones be filled with laughter, and that you speak to them as they worship with you during their worship services. Finally, Lord, I commit each of them to you, who is able to do for them above and beyond all that I ask or think, according to your power. To you, Lord, be the glory, honor and praise! Bless them mightily. Amen!

God bless!

"If you had a conversation with
the Lord right now,
what would He say to you?"

Abandoned Love

Scripture: *"But I have this against you: you have abandoned your first love."*

(Revelation 2:4 RSV)

DEVOTIONAL

When was the last time you did a personal inventory in regard to your relationship with the Lord? If you had a conversation with the Lord right now—today—would He say to you, as He said to the church at Ephesus, "You have abandoned your first love?" I don't know about you, but those are words that I don't ever want to hear from the Master. "You don't love me as much as you did when you first believed. What happened to you?" Notice, I didn't ask what happened to the Lord, because I can answer that for all of us! I asked, "What happened to you/me?" You see, my friends, the Lord loves us just as much and probably even more than when we first believed. The Lord's love is the same today, yesterday, and He hasn't changed. His priorities have not changed. His love for us has not changed. His caring for us has not changed. His watching over us has not changed. Our being his priority has not changed. The Lord hasn't changed, so if anyone has changed, it is you and I. He loves us and we are #1 on his list. But the question still remains, what about us? Is the Lord still #1 on our list, or has He been replaced with the cares of this world, such as money, job promotion, rising gas prices, fabulous homes, and so forth? Don't misunderstand me—these things are important—but never forget to, "seek ye FIRST the kingdom of heaven and its righteousness and all these other things will be added." Matthew 6:33 *emphasis mine*.

God bless!

"I know your tribulation and poverty, yet you are rich. . ."

Attitude

Scripture: *"I know your tribulation and poverty, yet you are rich."*
(Revelation 2:9 NIV)

DEVOTIONAL

This scripture is part of a conversation that Jesus had with one of his churches. He is sharing with them that He is aware of what is happening with them, what is happening around them, and also what they are about to go through. He makes an interesting statement to them. He says, "I know your tribulation and poverty, yet you are rich." He acknowledges that they are poverty stricken ... that they are experiencing tribulation ... and yet He says, "but you are rich." How can this be? How can one endure "tribulation" and be in "poverty," and yet be "rich?" I think the answer lies in one's attitude, one's viewpoint on life, and one's faith in God.

Attitude makes all the difference in the world for us Christians. If we see everything as hopeless, helpless, doom and gloom, then our circumstances will dictate our viewpoint on life. Likewise, it will trample our faith in God. Confusing? Let me explain! The late Rev. Dr. C.A.W. Clark used to say, "because one lives in the ghetto ... doesn't mean that one has to have ghetto thoughts." You may be living in poverty and you may be going through tribulation, but your attitude can be one of FAITH. You do not have to have a "ghetto thoughts" mentality!

This is what Paul meant when he said, "I have learned to be content in whatever circumstances I am." He didn't mean that he didn't care! He didn't mean that he didn't strive to make life better! He didn't mean that he quit or gave up! He meant that his circumstances did not dictate his attitude and his FAITH in God. Kind of like what Mother Teresa did. She lived in poverty in the streets of Calcutta, but no one would argue that she wasn't rich. She was indeed rich! She was rich in love! She was rich in her commitment to care for God's people regardless of their race, creed, color or national origin. I think Christ would look at her and say, "I know your tribulation and poverty, yet you are rich." What about you and me? Can He say the same thing about us?

Something to think about!

God bless!

Testimony

Scripture: *"I have been young and now I am old, yet I have not seen the righteous abandoned or his children begging bread."*
(Psalm 37:25 HCSB)

DEVOTIONAL

If I were to give this verse a title or a subject, I would call it, "The testimony of an old man." (Okay, okay, maybe not an old man but a senior statesman … smile!) At any rate, in this psalm, David gives a testimony or an account of his experience with God. David seems to be saying, as my dad used to say, "Experience is the best teacher, and my experience has taught me that God will and has ALWAYS come through for me." David's testimony is one of encouragement to his people as well as to us. For it is true, when I, too, look back over my life, I must stand in agreement with David, "I have never seen the righteous abandoned." Now, I'm not as old as David was, but I think I have enough of that "experience thing" to speak as he did. My experience has taught me, too, that God has never abandoned me as one of his righteous. Whether I was sailing across the Atlantic Ocean during a fierce storm, driving down the dangerous streets of Haiti, or flying through the unstable and dangerous skies of Iraq, God ALWAYS has protected and cared for me. And guess what? He has always taken care of you, too! "Always?" you ask. Yes, always! I invite you to email me one time when He hasn't! (I'll be waiting.)

The last thing that David says in this verse has to do with his children. He says that not only has his experience taught him that the righteous are not abandoned by God, but also that the righteous children have not had to beg for bread. When you and I live a righteous life before God, our children receive a blessing from God as well. They are protected by our righteousness. Does this mean that they will not make bad choices and have to suffer the consequences? No! Our children will be held accountable for the choices they make. However, my son, your son, your daughter, your children receive so many blessings because of your righteousness and your relationship before and with God. This should give all of us with children the incentive to do a few things:

(1) to live a righteous life before God,
(2) to pray for our children daily,
(3) to train them up in the ways of God, and
(4) to share with them how God has blessed, provided, and cared for us and them.

Man, this is good stuff! It's good to know that Nigell (my son) is living under the protection of God "partly" because of my relationship with God. Oh, by the way, I do remind him of it every now and then. You know what, I think he knows it!

God bless!

Enemies

Scripture: *"If your enemy is hungry, feed him. If he is thirsty, give him something to drink. For in so doing you will be heaping burning coals on his head."*

(Romans 12:19-21 NLT)

DEVOTIONAL

I must confess that this is one scripture that makes me laugh every time I read it and think about what Paul has said for us to do to our enemies. I have often imagined some people walking around slapping their heads from the burning coals. Just imagine for a moment someone taking a match, striking it, and then setting your hair on fire. Got the picture!? It's not a pretty sight. In fact, when you think about it, it's a painful sight. Yet this is what Paul says happens when we take the high ground (if you will) when it comes to dealing with our enemies. The good part about this scripture is that "it's the Lord who is striking the match (if you will) and setting our enemy's hair on fire." Now, why do I say that? "For it is written: 'Vengeance belongs to Me, I will repay,' says the Lord." You see, when we do as Paul says—"feed your enemy," "give water to your enemy," "do not be conquered by evil but conquer evil with good"—it sets the hair on top of our enemy's head a blazing (on fire, in other words). Do you want to hear something funny? I don't have hair! Therefore, if I were your enemy and you did the things to me that Paul recommended (feed me, give me water, don't try to conquer evil with evil but with good), you would set my scalp a blazing (on fire, in other words). So guess what? I am not your enemy and my scalp/head is off limits (smile).

When I/you try to get revenge on someone, or you and I try to fight our own battle, we will always have to fight it again. But, when God gets revenge...when God fights our battle...our enemy's head is set ablaze.

He/she will lose the battle and you and I will never have to fight the battle again. Why? Because when God gets revenge, it is final!

God bless!

Persistent Prayer

Scripture: *"Love must be without hypocrisy. Detest evil; cling to what is good. Rejoice in hope; be patient in affliction; be persistent in prayer...if possible, on your part, live in peace with everyone."*
(Romans 12: 9-18 HCSB)

DEVOTIONAL

The life of a Christian is definitely different and it's supposed to be. We are called to higher standards, more is expected of us, all eyes are on us ... and people are watching us daily to see if we are different from any Joe Schmuckatelli who walks down the street. As Christians, we are not supposed to be like everyone else, especially if everyone else is not walking in the ways of God.

Is this tough and difficult at times? You bet it is! But regardless of how tough or difficult it is, the life of a Christian stands out, and it should stand out in such a way that others will know, not only that we are different, but also that we belong to Christ. Listen to what the Apostle Paul said about how a Christian should be: "Love must be real (without hypocrisy); we are to detest evil and cling to what is good." In other words, we are to resent, hate, and despise evil to the point that it becomes sickness to us. On the other hand, we are to "cling" (hold on tight or have a strong emotional attachment) to what is good.

Doing what is right and good in God's eyesight should be much more important than doing what is right in our own eyesight. Does this mean that we will on occasion be falsely accused? Yes! Does this mean that on occasion we will be persecuted? Yes! Does this mean that on occasion we may be overlooked and not receive what we think we deserve? Yes! But Paul answers those questions this way, "Rejoice in hope; be patient in affliction; be persistent in prayer." If you don't mind, let me reverse the order just a bit: "be persistent in prayer!" Why do I reverse the order? I'm convinced that a persistent prayer life will aid one in "rejoicing in hope and being patient in affliction." I'm convinced that a persistent prayer life will aid one in accomplishing what Paul said to do in verse 18: "If possible, on your part, live at peace with everyone." The importance of a persistent prayer life cannot be overstated. It is crucial! If you do not have a persistent prayer life, I encourage you to start one NOW!

God bless!

Criticism

Scripture*: "Therefore, let us no longer criticize one another."*
(Romans 14:13 HCSB)

DEVOTIONAL

Now, here's an interesting thought. "Let us no longer criticize one another." HUM! Can you imagine what it would be like to go through (just) one day without criticizing someone? I don't just mean verbally. I mean in our thoughts as well. For remember, Proverbs 23:7 says, "For as he thinks within himself, so he is." We may think that our thoughts are not important but they are. Jesus said, "Everyone who looks at a woman to lust for her has already committed adultery with her in his heart" (Matthew 5:28). Yes, our thoughts do matter. I have been asked the question many times. Is it better to think about something and not do it or to think about it and do it? I usually give the same answer. When it comes to breaking God's law, it is better to do neither. If it is wrong, don't think about it and DON'T DO IT! It doesn't have to be either; it can be both. In other words, we can train our thoughts! We can set our mind and/or heart on things above! We can say, "let the mind be in me that was in Christ Jesus." Does it take discipline? Yes, it does! Does it take a determination? Yes, it does! Does it take (what I talked about yesterday) persistent prayer? Yes, it does! But we can do it. We can use determination to avoid criticizing one another. Here is one way not to criticize: don't take part in those conversations when others are doing it. What do you think? Join me today in having a "no criticizing day."

God bless!

"Have you ever met or seen any 'too-salty' Christians?"

Salt

Scripture: *"You are the salt of the earth. But if the salt should lose its taste, how can it be made salty? It's no longer good for anything but to be thrown out and trampled on by men."*

(Matthew 5: 13 NLT)

DEVOTIONAL

Salt is an interesting commodity. It can be good and it can be bad. It all depends upon how one uses it and how much of it one uses. Salt, as you know, can add flavor or it can make you frown. It can be used to season your food or it can be used to cure a bad sore throat. When seasoning your food, if you put too much salt on your meal it becomes uneatable—too salty. Have you ever met or seen any "too-salty" Christians? I have, and they were hard to stomach. They wore a cross around their neck, but they had no joy in their life. They had a Bible on their desk, but they never opened it. Or they read their Bible daily (yes daily), but they did not show compassion as the words in the Bible teach. They don't lie, cheat, steal and more, but they have a very unforgiving spirit and they are quick to point out the faults of everyone else but themselves. They have the outward appearance of being a "salty Christian," but the problem is that they have lost their taste. I don't know about you but I want to be an effective salty Christian— one whom others can see, smell and taste the Christ within. I don't want to be in that group described this way by Jesus: you have lost your taste and therefore you are "no longer good for anything but to be thrown out and trampled on by men." What about you? Are you an effective salty Christian or are you an ineffective too-salty Christian and therefore no longer good?

God bless!

Statute of Christ the Redeemer in Rio de Janerio, Brazil.

Faithfulness

Scripture: *"Please Lord, remember how I have walked before You faithfully and wholeheartedly and have done what is good in Your sight."*

(2 Kings 20: 3 HCSB)

DEVOTIONAL

If you ever doubt that there is a reason to live a faithful life and to live for the Lord with your whole heart, please read 2 Kings 20: 1-6. This testimony of King Hezekiah gives me goose bumps. (I know, here I go again with these goose bumps statements.) But it's true. I feel them right now. At any rate, Isaiah the prophet had delivered a fatal message to King Hezekiah. Isaiah informed Hezekiah that God had revealed that the king should set his house in order, for Hezekiah was about to die.

Now, I'm sure this news didn't make Hezekiah happy, and he may have been a bit puzzled or even a bit sad. However, listen to how King Hezekiah responded. "He turned his face to the wall" and said to the Lord, "Lord, remember how I have walked before you faithfully and wholeheartedly and have done what is good in your sight."

Hezekiah didn't give up. He didn't pout. He didn't fall into a deep state of depression. Instead, he reminded God about how he had lived and how he had served Him faithfully. He called God's attention to his life! But that's the kind of relationship that King Hezekiah had with God. He could do this because he had dedicated his life to serving and pleasing God. In other words, he had built up what I call "dividends" with the Lord, and he was (if you will) cashing them in. Hezekiah reminded God that he had served Him "wholeheartedly" and "faithfully" and was asking God to change his mind and allow him to live longer. He was serious. He was so serious that he "wept," and because of his faithfulness ... because of his love for God ... because he had spent his life "doing what was good in God's sight," God changed his mind. He sent the prophet Isaiah back to King Hezekiah with these words, "I have heard your prayer; I have seen your tears. Look, I will heal you. I will add 15 years to your life. I will deliver you and this city from the hand of the King of Assyria." In other words, because of Hezekiah's life—his life of serving God and doing what was right in God's sight—he made God change his mind. God not only added more years to his life, but He delivered him from the hands of his enemies.

Now, just think about that for a moment and then tell me that you are not feeling those goose bumps. You see, my friends, when you live a faithful and wholehearted life for God, you will build up dividends, and God will allow you to cash them in every now and then, as He did with King Hezekiah.

God bless!

Rest

Scripture: *"God completed His work that He had done, and He rested."*

(Genesis 2:2 HCSB)

DEVOTIONAL

Many people would say that I'm a workaholic, and there probably is some truthfulness to their claim. I very often have to remind myself that I'm not that important, I'm not indispensible, and life will most definitely go on if I'm not around to handle everything. There have been times when (even while at home trying to sleep), I find myself doing several things that keep me from resting and from getting a good night's sleep. Some of these things include the following. (1) I replay the things of the day. I can't go back and change a thing, so I may as well let it go and handle it the next day. (2) I allow my mind to race at a very fast pace, thinking about what I have to do the next day, therefore, losing much needed sleep. I wake up tired and not refreshed from the day before, and I am still too tired to do a good job the current day. (3) I stay up too late trying to complete the things that I didn't finish and getting frustrated and still not getting a good night's sleep (sound familiar?). The bottom line is that I need to take a lesson from the creator, God. He created the world in seven days and then He RESTED. He prioritized his time, planned out the schedule of what He was going to do each day, stuck with the plan, and completed the planned work in six days. Then He rested from ALL his work.

My prayer for all of us today is that we, too, will REST from all our work as God did when He created the world and us.

God bless!

"I don't try to live
for the approval of others."

Honor

Scripture: *"We are careful to be honorable before the Lord, but we also want everyone else to know we are honorable."*

(2 Corinthians 8:21 NLT)

DEVOTIONAL

I have been preaching for over 29 years and if there is one thing that I have learned, it is that perception does count and it can hurt one's ministry. I don't try to live for the approval of others, but I do try to live in such a way that others can approve of me, if they choose. In today's scripture reading, Paul alludes to this kind of thinking as well. He says, "We are careful to be honorable before the Lord, but we also want everyone else to know that we are honorable." Paul was so determined to keep down suspicion and to live honorably before God and people that he sent more than one person to Jerusalem to deliver the offering (money, collection) to the Jerusalem church. He wanted to be sure that no one could accuse him and his followers of anything other than living honorably before God and before one another. We, too, would be wise to live in such a way that will not only bring honor to our Lord, but will also enable others to see that we are honorable. This means, as 1 Thessalonians 5:17 says, "staying away from the appearance of evil."

God bless!

"What I want instead is your true thanks to God."

Thankfulness

Scripture*: "O My people, listen as I speak. Here are My charges against you, O Israel.... What I want instead is your true thanks to God; I want you to fulfill your vows to the Most High. Trust me in your times of trouble, and I will rescue you, and you will give me glory."*

(Psalm 50: 7-15 NLT)

DEVOTIONAL

I have been asked many times, what does God want me to do for Him? What is my calling? What am I to do in this life to glorify God? Well, Psalm 50: 7-15 goes a long way in telling us what God wants from all of us. Listen to God's words:

O My people, listen as I speak. Here are My charges against you, O Israel; I am God, your God! I have no complaint about your sacrifices or the burnt offerings you constantly bring to My altar. But I want no more bulls from your barns; I want no more goats from your pens. For all the animals of the forest are mine and I own the cattle on a thousand hills. Every bird of the mountains and all the animals of the field belong to me. If I were hungry, I would not mention it to you, for all the world is mine and everything in it. I don't need the bulls you sacrifice; I don't need the blood of goats. What I want instead is your true thanks to God; I want you to fulfill your vows to the Most High. Trust me in your times of trouble, and I will rescue you, and you will give me glory.

You see my friends, God's request is simple! He says through the psalmist that He wants three things from us: (1) our true thanks to God; (2) for us to fulfill our vows to the Most High; (3) for us to trust

Him in times of trouble. The benefits of doing those three things are that (1) God will rescue you/us from whatever we need rescuing from, and (2) we will give God glory. WOW!

God bless!

Cheerful Giving

Scripture: *"Remember this – a farmer who plants only a few seeds will get a small crop. But the one who plants generously will get a generous crop.... For God loves the person who gives cheerfully. And God will generously provide all you need."*

(2 Corinthians 9: 6-7 NLT)

DEVOTIONAL

In case you didn't know, I'm a Baptist minister! As such, I am often teased about two things: (1) Baptist preachers love to eat, and (2) Baptist preachers love money. Well, I am definitely guilty of the first one, but I don't think I fall into the category of loving money. I do, however, love to give. I love to give because God has so graciously given to me. I love to give because I know what it is like to live on the verge of bankruptcy. I love to give because when I was at the lowest point financially, I made God a promise: if He blessed me financially, I would never stop giving. Also, and what's more important, I promised that I would give "cheerfully." The only thing I asked God to do for me in return was to bless me with a "joy of giving" spirit and that I would be able to bless someone else. When I went through my financial hardship, God changed my attitude toward giving, toward money, and toward what was most important to Him as well as to me. You see, my brothers and sisters, I want to be one of those farmers Paul talks about. The farmer "who plants generously will get a generous crop" from God. But here is the key to this giving concept, according to Paul: you must love it and you must do it cheerfully." Why? It's because "God loves the person who gives cheerfully. And God will generously provide all you need." Oh, by the way, this concept doesn't just apply to money, but it applies to life in general. Got you! You thought I was only talking about money. No, I'm talking about giving, PERIOD! Whatever God has blessed you with, share it "cheerfully" and "lovingly."

God bless!

"... if you run with dogs,
you will get fleas."

Negativity

Scripture: *"Keep away from angry, short-tempered people, or you will learn to be like them and endanger your soul."*
(Proverbs 22: 24-25 NLT)

DEVOTIONAL

In the area where I grew up in (Coldwater, Mississippi), people would say, "If you run with dogs, you will get fleas." In this day and time, if you quoted that phrase, someone would probably say, "Yes, but if you use some type of Frontline repellent, the fleas won't stick to you." I'm not sure either is true. However, in Proverbs 22: 24-25, the writer warns us to "keep away from angry, short-tempered people, or you will learn to be like them." I do know from personal experience that the more I hang around negative people, the more I hang out with angry and/or short-tempered people, the more I hang out with people who do not bring out the best in me—that is the Christ in me—the more negative, angry, and short-tempered I become. Now, maybe you are different, or maybe you're not but you just don't want to admit it. The truth of the matter is that the words of the writer in Proverbs 22: 24-25 are true for all of us. The more we hang around angry and/or short-tempered people the more we become angry and short-tempered. This is one scripture that I won't ask you to test, because I don't want you to lose what you have or what God has delivered you from. I will close by saying this: be on guard against those around you who are always negative, those who always produce a negative spirit, those who always find the worst in everyone, and those who never have anything good to say about anybody. Be on guard because you will be next. You will find yourself doing the very same things that you hate about the person who is doing them. So as the word says, "be watchful" for a little yeast can spoil the whole batch.

God bless!

"I'm sure that when you reflect on that day, it will (even now) bring tears of joy to your eyes."

Savior's Day

Scripture: *"In the year King Uzziah died, I (Isaiah) saw the Lord. He was sitting on a lofty throne, and the train of his robe filled the Temple."*

(Isaiah 6:1 NLT)

DEVOTIONAL

Can you remember when you had your first encounter with the Lord? Did a special event happen in the world on your special day of meeting the Lord? Do you associate, as Isaiah did, your first encounter with the Lord with a certain moment? Think about it. Where were you when God spoke to your heart? Why do I ask you to do this? This should be one day that lives in your memory forever. This was the first day of the rest of your life. It was a day that God delivered you from darkness to light, and I'm sure that when you reflect on that day, it will (even now) bring tears of joy to your eyes.

Isaiah described his day in this way: "He [the Lord] was sitting on a lofty throne, and the train of his robe filled the Temple." What a powerful image! I don't know it to be true, but I bet you that every time Isaiah reflected on his special day of meeting the Lord (here we go again ... you got it), those famous goose bumps just filled his heart. As I reflect right now on that day when Christ came into my heart, it brings joy to my heart, puts a smile on my face, and (yes) gives me goose bumps all over. I can remember it like it was yesterday! I won't go into details, but I assure you that when Christ came into my heart, He changed me, my surroundings, and my outlook on life. What about you? Take a moment right now and reflect upon your special day. Then, for the rest of this day, occasionally think about what the Lord did for you on that day when He came into your heart. When you do this today, all those other small things won't matter!

God bless!

Subversive Plots

Scripture: *"Do not think like everyone else does. Do not be afraid that some plan conceived behind closed doors will be the end of you."*

(Isaiah 8: 11-14 NLT)

DEVOTIONAL

Have you ever allowed yourself to become concerned about plans of others to do you harm? Don't be! Have you worked at a place and felt that your co-workers were trying their best to set you up, get you fired, make you look bad in the eyes of your boss and others? Don't worry about it! Have you heard of others talking behind your back, gossiping about you, plotting to overthrow you, leaving you out of important decisions, or keeping important information from you? Don't lose a minute of sleep over it! Listen to the prophet Isaiah and be encouraged TODAY: "Do not think like everyone else does. Do not be afraid that some plan conceived behind closed doors will be the end of you. Do not fear anything except the Lord Almighty. He alone is the Holy One. If you fear Him [in other words give Him reverence], you need fear nothing else. He will keep you safe." After we read these verses, the only thing left to be said is, "Amen!"

God bless!

Chaplain King preaches in Tanzania at a local Assemblies of God Church.

The Medium

Scripture: *"So why are you trying to find out the future by consulting mediums and psychics? Do not listen to their whisperings and mutterings. Can the living find out the future from the dead? Why not ask your God?"*

(Isaiah 8:19 NLT)

DEVOTIONAL

I have often said to myself and others, "if I want to know something, I will ask God." If God will tell a medium and psychic something about me or you (and I'm not saying that He would), then He will also tell you and me, and it will not cost us a penny. I can save my money by going to the very same source that a medium or psychic goes to in order to find out something about me or my future. The door to the heart and mind of God is open to you and me just as it is to anyone else. The only thing you have to do is to ASK! Ask God yourself what you want to know about your future! Ask God yourself what His plans are for your life! Ask God yourself if you should marry a particular person! Ask God yourself if this is the right guy/gal for you! Ask God yourself whether or not you should buy or invest in a certain thing! He will tell you! Now, if you must give your money away, then give it to me. However, don't give me your money because you want God to tell me something about your life. Give it to me because you just want to give me your money! Otherwise, keep your money in your pocket and don't waste it by going to mediums and psychics to find out what God will tell you Himself! Remember what Isaiah said, "Why not ask your God?"

God bless!

"We must be very careful
that we do not get caught up
in our own selves."

False Credit

Scripture*: "After the Lord has used the king of Assyria to accomplish his purposes in Jerusalem, he will turn against the king of Assyria and punish him—for he is proud and arrogant. He boasts, 'By my own power and wisdom I have won these wars. By my own strength I have captured many lands, destroyed their kings, and carried off their treasures.... No one can even flap a wing against me or utter a peep of protest.'"*

(Isaiah 10: 12-14 NLT)

DEVOTIONAL

It's a dangerous thing to take credit for what God has done for you. When we do that, we border on being prideful and arrogant, and God doesn't like either pride or arrogance. We must be very careful that we do not get caught up in our own selves, our own abilities, or our own egos. We must always realize that it's not by our power or by our might, but it's by God's spirit that we are what we are and who we are—and that we have accomplished the things that we have accomplished. As recorded in today's scripture reading, God used the enemy of Israel to accomplish His purpose, but clearly stated that He would (afterward) defeat the Assyrians (Israel's enemy) because of their pride and arrogance. Because the King of Assyria took credit for what God did, he and his people paid the price by bringing down the wrath of God and losing all that was accomplished. We, too, must be careful that we do not take credit for God's victories. Remember this phrase: To God be the glory for the great things "He" has done!

God bless!

Chaplain King visits with religious leaders from Comoros.

The Student

Scripture: "A student is not greater than the teacher. A servant is not greater than the master.... And since I, the master of the household, have been called the prince of demons, how much more will it happen to you."

(Matthew 10: 24-25 NLT)

DEVOTIONAL

Recently, I was reminded of how it feels when one blatantly lies about you. In fact, I found myself feeling emotions that I had not felt in quite some time. Then I found myself falling for that ancient old trick of Satan: "feeling sorry for myself" and developing a "poor little me" attitude. But then God did to me what He so often does. He reminded me of his Son and how his one and only Son was treated by those who called themselves religious. Additionally, God reminded me that I am no more than "my teacher Jesus" and that I am not greater than my Master (Jesus), whom I serve. Jesus was perfect in every sense of the word, and He only "went about doing good," and yet He was lied about, talked about, ridiculed, and ultimately nailed to a cross. When I put in context the things that I have to endure (being lied about) and compare these to what our savior had to go through for you and me, I shake off the "feeling sorry for myself" as well as the "poor little me" attitude. To be honest, I feel ashamed to complain about the little irritants that I have to endure when Jesus endured the cross for me. Wow! Thanks, Lord, for reminding me (and all of us) that "a student is not greater than the teacher [You, Lord] and a servant is not greater than the master [You, Lord]."

God bless!

"One who is most patient
is also gentle
with his/her tongue."

Gentleness

Scripture*: "Through Patience a Ruler can be persuaded, and a gentle tongue can break a bone."*

(Proverbs 25:15 NIV)

DEVOTIONAL

There's a saying that goes like this, "patience is a virtue that we all must possess." Lord, how true this statement is, especially when it comes to getting along with others (and to be honest, getting along with myself as well). One needs patience in dealing with others who are not kind, others who are selfish, and others who rub us the wrong way. Patience is a trait that is good to have, PERIOD. It can save you from much headache and heartache! It can assist you in not taking things personally, even though a thing may be personal! It can help you (and this one is good for me personally) to overlook the ego or attitude of another and prevent you from losing sleep over trivial matters! It can keep you from "majoring in the minors" and "minoring in the majors!" To be honest, PATIENCE can help you save money on medicine and help you avoid many unhealthy things! In today's proverb, the writer introduces us to another kind of patience. It is a persistent kind of patience that persuades a ruler (or leader). A gentle tongue goes along with such patience. I have discovered that the more patient I am, the more compassionate and gentle I am in dealing with others. These two virtues go hand-in-hand! A good argument can be made (at least for me) that one who is patient is also gentle with his/her tongue. Isn't this true of our Lord and Savior? He is most patient with us, and He breaks all bones with his gentle tongue. Thank you, Lord, for showing us what patience really means!

God bless!

Chaplain King holds a girl at the baby orphanage in Djibouti, Africa.

Blessedness

Scripture: *"Blessed are the poor in spirit, because the kingdom of heaven is theirs."*

(Matthew 5:3 HCSB)

DEVOTIONAL

From the very beginning Jesus was different from the norm! His teachings were different. His message was different. His attitude was different. His outlook was different. His dealing with people was different. He was not your normal (in the traditional sense of the word) kind of guy. He calls all of us to a higher cause greater than self, and He asks us to do things that we are not accustomed to doing. Such is the case when He spoke the words, "Blessed [or happy] are the poor in spirit." The term "poor," as Jesus is using it, has a double meaning. It suggests both poverty and humility. The poor are those who have nothing and hope only in God. Blessed (or happy) are those who are poverty stricken, for their hope is in God. They depend upon God for everything. They are not happy to be in poverty, but they are not consumed by their situation for their hope is in God. Also, blessed are those who are "not" in poverty, for they are humble, and their hope, too, is in God. They, too, depend upon God for everything, and they have a spirit of humility. So Jesus is saying that whether people are poor or rich—in poverty or not in poverty—they are *blessed* as long as their hope, trust, and faith are only in God.

God bless!

"The issue for us now is
not whether we 'know' the way,
but whether
we will 'follow' the way."

The Navigator

Scripture: *"Look, I am sending My messenger ahead of You, who will prepare Your way."*

(Mark 1:2 HCSB)

DEVOTIONAL

Have you ever tried to find a particular place without a map and become lost? Your memory failed you, and what you thought you remembered, you had forgotten. Feeling lost is terrible, especially when you are not familiar with the area or your surroundings. Such is not the case when it comes to the highway to heaven or the way to God. God is so good, so gracious, so loving, so thoughtful, and so kind that He sent one with the "perfect" road map, and therefore, the way has been laid out and prepared. The way is so plain and the road map is so easy to read that even a "not so smart" guy like me can read it and understand it. The issue for us now is not whether we "know" the way, but whether we will "follow" the way that the messenger has laid out for us. Think of the map example again. If we have a road map and choose not to follow it and in turn end up lost, whose fault is it? Is it the map's fault? Of course not! I think we all can agree that it is either reader's error or a failure to use the road map provided. So what's the point? I'm glad you asked! The point is that God has sent his Son, Jesus, as a messenger and He (Jesus) has prepared the way for us. He has prepared the way of Salvation. He has prepared the way of Peace. He has prepared the way of Righteousness. He has prepared the way of Love. The bottom line is that He did it all, and He did it just for you and me! We have no excuse! If we miss the mark or the way, it's our fault!

God bless!

Chaplain King with children in refugee camp in Uganda.

End Times

Scripture: *"Woe because of that day! For the Day of the Lord is near and will come as devastation from the Almighty."*

(Joel 1: 15 HCSB)

DEVOTIONAL

Many books have been written on the end times and the return of the Lord. Many preachers, teachers, scholars, Bible readers, and a host of others spend a lot to time trying to determine just when the Lord will return. Well, I'll be the first to admit that I don't have the answer to this question. Often, when people discover I am a minister, they ask, "So do you think we are in the last days?" or "Do you think the world is going to end soon?" I usually say, "I don't know, and to be honest, I don't spend a lot of time thinking about it." When I give this answer, many people stop and give me a strange stare. I'm not sure why, but my guess is that they are a little taken aback by my answer. I spend very little time thinking about when the end will be or when the Lord will return, because I try to live every day as though it is my last day. I try to be prepared for the Lord's return regardless of when his return will be. I'm convinced that the scriptures dealing with the last days and the end of time are given for our education. We should not focus so much attention on when the last days will happen. If we live our lives as the Master has taught, stay ready at all times (as the scripture says "be ye always ready"), live for Christ daily, and follow His teachings always, then the timing of the end will be less important than doing all we can, as much as we can, and as often as we can for the Lord, now.

God bless!

"They did all the right things,
but for the wrong reasons."

Self-Centeredness

Scripture: *"Everything they do is done for men to see."*
(Matthew 23:5 NIV)

DEVOTIONAL

Why do you wear a cross? Why do you have your Bible out on your desk? Why do you have Christian phrases on your car? Why do you go to church, Bible study or Sunday school? These may seem like strange questions, but they really are not. You see, in today's devotion, Jesus is confronting those who do things for self-glorification, bringing attention to self and highlighting what they are all about. It is clear that the Lord does not approve or want us to be all about self. He wants us to be about Him! His statement seems very clear: "Everything they do is done for men to see." Were these religious folks? Some of them were! Were these Bible readers? Yes, some of them were! Were these folks who wore religious objects? Yes, they were! But in spite of what they appeared to be (religious), Christ warned us to do what they *said* rather than what they actually *did*. These folks did not practice what they preached. They did all the right things, but for the wrong reasons. "They did it for men to see." What about you and me? Why do we do the things that we do? I'm not sure about you, but I want to make sure that what I do in the public (read my Bible, wear my cross, show my Christian bumper stickers and so on) is done for Christ and "not to be seen or praised by you or anyone else." Think about it!

God bless!

Vice Admiral Ann E. Rondeau, president of the National Defense University, congratulates Chaplain King.

Belief

Scripture*: "As a result, they would carry the sick out into the streets and lay them on beds and pallets so that when Peter came by, at least his shadow might fall on some of them."*

(Acts 5:15 HCSB)

DEVOTIONAL

What is the difference between now and what happened in the days of Jesus and the apostles? Today's scripture depicts a wonderful and powerful thing. The people carried their sick into the streets for the apostles to heal them. When they couldn't get close enough for the apostle to touch them or to pay special attention to them, they placed their loved ones and/or friends in the path where Peter would walk so that "his shadow might fall on some of them." This is deep! They were so adamant about getting help for their loved ones that they wanted Peter's shadow to fall on them so that they would be healed. Well, what was the difference between then and now? Only one difference—they believed it could be done! In other words, when they took their friends and/or loved ones out into the street to see Peter, they believed in their hearts that Peter could not only heal the sick, but also that the mere touch of his "shadow" (falling upon them) could heal them. I can hear the question coming from some of you now, "Can this happen in today's time?" Well, here is the answer back to you. Yes, it can! It can because of one's faith and it can because of one's belief. Remember, Jesus said, "Whatever you ask in My name believing it shall be done." The difference is "my" faith in what I ask Him (Christ) to do for me. Oh, by the way, when you read this email and/or this "Thought for the Day," don't dissect what I'm saying with "reason," just believe it in "faith." Thanks!

God bless!

"Are you willing to lay it all on the altar?"

Trust

Scripture: *"For now I know that you fear God, since you have not withheld your only son from me."*

(Genesis 22:12 HCSB)

DEVOTIONAL

Just how far will you go to obey God? Are you willing to lay it all on the altar and allow God to "totally" run, control, or direct your life? I tell you, when you come to this point in your life and in your relationship with God, it is not only a beautiful thing; it is "freedom." Is it a little scary at times? You bet it is, but if you work and pray at totally allowing God to run, control, and direct your life, you will have "Peace which surpasses all understanding." Really, I'm serious. You really will! I'm not joking. When you can do as Abraham did—be willing to follow God's directions even when it seems crazy to do so—you will have inner peace, outer peace, and total peace.

In today's scripture reading, God told Abraham to take his only son and offer him as a sacrifice to God. Abraham did what God told him to do. Just at the point when he was ready to make the sacrifice, God called out to him: "Do not lay a hand on the boy or do anything to him. For now, I know that you fear God, since you have not withheld your only son from me." We know from reading Abraham's life story in Genesis that his life took off from this point onward and that God did things for him that He has not done for anyone else since. He blessed Abraham; he blessed Abraham's seed and/or descendants; he blessed Abraham's finances; he blessed Abraham's entire household; he blessed everything that Abraham touched ... all because Abraham was willing to lay it all on the altar and to TOTALLY trust God to the fullest. Now, before you panic, don't worry, God is not going to ask you to offer up your child to him for a sacrifice. Why? Because you are not Abraham and that is not your calling. He might, however, ask you to offer up your job, your friendship, your finances, your whatever, to see just how far you will go to obey and to trust Him. He might ask you to offer up that one thing in your life that is hindering you from TOTALLY trusting Him. He might ask you to offer up that one thing that has become your God and that you have replaced him with. Remember His words, "I am a jealous God and they shall have no other God before Me."

God bless!

Anger Management

Scripture: *"For his anger lasts only a moment, but his favor lasts a lifetime!"*

(Psalm 30:4-5 NIV)

DEVOTIONAL

Unresolved anger will kill you! It will kill your personality. It will kill your positive outlook on life. It will kill your surroundings. It will kill everything you touch, if you allow it to go unchecked or unresolved. Anger is natural and normal! Anyone who expects to go through life and not get angry is not being realistic. To get angry is not sinful. However, how we respond when we get angry makes all the difference in the world. The scripture reading for today says, "For his anger lasts only a moment." The psalmist is saying that God gets angry, but in the fourth verse we are encouraged to "sing to the Lord" and to "praise his holy name." Why would the psalmist encourage us to sing to God when the Lord is angry? One reason is because God doesn't stay angry forever, and He doesn't stay angry long. He doesn't hold it in (so to speak), and He doesn't allow it to build up. He gets angry when I sin against Him. He gets angry when I disobey his word. Yes, God gets angry for a "moment," but don't be discouraged, my friends, because "his favor lasts a lifetime." His anger last only for a moment, but you and I have his favor forever. Praise the Lord that God doesn't hold grudges the way we do. We get angry and stay angry for years. God gets angry and it last only for a moment. THANK GOD!

God bless!

Chaplain King with religious leaders at EID dinner in Mauritius.

Satisfaction

Scripture: *"But when all goes well for you, remember that I was with you. Please show kindness to me by mentioning me to Pharaoh, and get me out of this prison."*

(Genesis 40: 14-15 HCSB)

DEVOTIONAL

Early in my military career, I was overlooked for an assignment that I thought I should have received. Anger, hurt, and disappointment were some of the emotions that I felt at the time. I decided to speak with a friend and mentor about the situation. I will never forget his words: "Bloom where you are." In other words, don't get hung up on the job you have been assigned or given, just bloom in the job that you have. After reading about Joseph's prison experience, I'm convinced that he had a "bloom where you are" attitude. Even though Joseph was in prison, he used the gift (interpretation of dreams) that God had blessed him with to bless others. I'm sure it was discouraging at times to stay upbeat, focused, and motivated and to do the will of God. However, in spite of his circumstances in prison, he bloomed where he was. As a result of doing so, God freed him from prison, elevated him to the second most powerful job in Egypt, and allowed him to ride in the second chariot. He was the secretary of state for all of Egypt and no one saw the king without seeing Joseph first. My friends, regardless of what job you have or what situation you are in, "bloom where you are."

God bless!

"A lived sermon will
go much farther than a
word only sermon."

Open Hearts

Scripture: *"These people say they are mine. They honor me with their lips, but their hearts are far away. And their worship of me amounts to nothing more than human laws learned by rote."*

(Isaiah 29:13 NLT)

Devotional

Which group are you in: the "lip service group" or "the phony worship group?" Today's scripture reading clearly shows us that God is not interested in lip service or phony worship. He is from the "show me" group and He wants to see your/my actions rather than to hear your/my words. In the words of the old saying, "A lived sermon will go much farther than a word only sermon."

Whether we realize it or not, people pay close attention not only to what we say but also to how we live. God is saying through the prophet Isaiah that his people (the children of Israel) honor Him "with their lips but their hearts are far away." The psalmist said much the same thing when he said the Lord delights in a broken and contrite spirit rather than in sacrifices. You see, my friends, we can talk all we like. We can go to church as much as we like. We can put on a religious appearance as much as we like. We can have people say nice things about us as much as possible, but the true test of a Man/Woman of God is whether a person honors God with his/her heart. God is not interested in your lip service and your worship that "amounts to nothing more than human laws learned by rote." He is interested in your heart and when you/we give Him our heart we will serve Him, not with lip service, but with true service. Our worship will be holy and pure, not phony and empty. Think about it! I am praying for you!

God bless!

The chapel where Chaplain King conducted worship service in Al Asad, Iraq.

True Blessedness

Scripture: *"My people will live in safety, quietly at home. They will be at rest. Even though the forest will be destroyed and the city torn down, God will greatly bless his people. Wherever they plant seed, bountiful crops will spring up. Their flocks and herds will graze in green pastures."*

(Isaiah 32:18-20 NLT)

DEVOTIONAL

The people to whom the prophet Isaiah was speaking were living in critical and crucial times. They were dealing with high gas prices, foreclosures of homes, failing banks. Businesses were closing at an alarming rate, corruption was at an all-time high, and the economy was bad—real bad. In spite of all these things, however, listen again to what God said through the prophet to his people: "My people will live in safety, quietly at home. They will be at rest. Even though the forest will be destroyed and the city torn down, God will greatly bless his people. Wherever they plant seed, bountiful crops will spring up. Their flocks and herds will graze in green pastures."

Of course the people of Isaiah's day didn't have cars, trucks, or automobiles. They didn't have high gas prices or insolvent banks. Businesses were not going out of business nor was anyone filing for bankruptcy. They were, however, living in perilous times and things for them were looking pretty bleak and bad. Yet the word of God came to encourage them at the right time, at the right moment, and just in time. Be encouraged today. Whatever the tide, God will take care of you!

Stay tuned for part 2. Tomorrow I will share more of what God said through his prophet!

God bless!

"Be strong, and do not fear,
for your God is coming
to destroy your enemies."

Fearlessness

Scripture: *"With this news, strengthen those who have tired hands, and encourage those who have weak knees. Say to those who are afraid, Be strong, and do not fear, for your God is coming to destroy your enemies. He is coming to save you."*

(Isaiah 35: 3-10 NLT)

DEVOTIONAL

As I stated in yesterday's "Thought for the Day," Isaiah was preaching during a time when things were bad. However, God instructed him, as He (God) is instructing me, to encourage the people. Tell them not to lose hope, not to lose heart, and not to lose faith. Regardless of the high gas prices and the failing economy, tell them this good news: "Be strong, and do not fear, for your God is coming to destroy your enemies. He is coming to save you." Wow! Isn't it awesome to know that regardless of what is happening in the world around us, OUR GOD is in control and He assures us that we are under his protective and loving care? Listen, my brothers and sisters, to the entire word for today. Listen to what God is saying through me to you today as I share with you his words of encouragement:

With this news, strengthen those who have weak knees. Say to those who are afraid, "Be strong, and do not fear, for your God is coming to destroy your enemies. He is coming to save you." And when He comes, He will open the eyes of the blind and unstop the ears of the deaf. The lame will leap like a deer, and those who cannot speak will shout and sing! Springs will gush forth in the wilderness, and streams will water the desert. The parched ground will become a pool, and springs of water will satisfy the thirsty land. Marsh grass and reeds and rushes will flourish where desert jackals once lived. Sorrow and mourning will disappear, and they will be overcome with joy and gladness.

The bottom line is this: your wilderness experience is temporary! Your sadness will be turned to joy and gladness! Your time of depression is about to end! Your season of hope and prosperity is at the door! Open it up now and let it all come in!

God bless!

Promise

Scripture: *"'For I know the plans I have for you,' declares the Lord, 'plans to prosper you and not to harm you, plans to give you hope and a future. Then you will call upon me and come and pray to me, and I will listen to you. You will seek me and find me when you seek me with all your heart.'"*

(Jeremiah 29:11-14 NIV)

DEVOTIONAL

As I thought about the word of God as He spoke through the prophet Jeremiah, I couldn't help but to tear up a bit. To think that God has a plan for me/for you, and the plan that He has cannot be canceled by anyone. When God makes a promise, He keeps it! When we make a promise, we very often break the promise, renege on the promise, forget that we made the promise, or just don't honor the promise at all. But, my friends, God's promise is true, sound, safe; you can take it to the bank and cash the check. The funds are guaranteed to be there and the failing economy has nothing to do with the promise of God. And guess what? Neither does any man, woman or anything. God's promise is solid.

So first of all, take stock in the fact that (1) God has a plan for your life; (2) his plan is for you to prosper; (3) his plan is not to harm you (see, I'm tearing up again); (3) your future from God is one of hope; (4) you have the right and the ability to call on God and the assurance that He will listen; (5) when you seek God, you will find Him. What a *powerful* assurance! What a *blessing* to be able to have the five things that I have listed for you and that God has promised you and that God will give and do for you.

Read the promise again: "'For I know the plans I have for you,' declares the Lord, 'plans to prosper you and not to harm you, plans to give you hope and a future. Then you will call upon me and come and pray to me, and I will listen to you. You will seek me and find me.'" My brothers and sisters, all these things are promised to us and the only thing that God requires is for us "to seek Him with all your heart." Now, I don't know about you, but I'm going to take Him up on His offer. I'm going to live in the freedom of his plans for me and for my life. Also, I will continue to seek and to love Him with all my heart.

God bless!

Omnipotence

Scripture*: "O Israel how can you say the Lord does not see your troubles? How can you say God refuses to hear your case? Have you never heard or understood?"*

(Isaiah 40:27-31 NLT)

DEVOTIONAL

As you have heard me say before, there are times when God's word doesn't need an explanation—it only needs to be read and for us to allow God to speak to us. Read the following scripture. It will minister to you, encourage your heart, settle your mind, and uplift your spirit.

> O Israel, how can you say the Lord does not see your troubles? How can you say God refuses to hear your case? Have you never heard or understood? Don't you know that the Lord is the everlasting God, the Creator of all the earth? He never grows faint or weary. No one can measure the depths of his understanding. He gives power to those who are tired and worn out; He offers strength to the weak. Even youths will become exhausted, and young men will give up. But those who wait on the Lord will find NEW [caps mine] strength. They will fly high on wings like eagles. They will run and not grow weary. They will walk and not faint.

And all the people said, "Amen."

God bless!

"Go to church and PRAY."

God's Temple

Scripture: *"When King Hezekiah heard their report, he tore his cloths and put on sackcloth and went into the temple of the Lord to pray."*

(Isaiah 37:1 NLT)

DEVOTIONAL

Where do you go when you need comforting? Where do you go when your enemies are threatening you? Where do you go when the pressures of life are weighing you down and closing in upon you? Let me make a suggestion and a recommendation: go to church and PRAY. Some will say, "Well, I can pray where I am and there is no need to go to church." Well, I beg to differ! It is true, you can pray anywhere. You can pray where you are. But there is something about going to God's house that seems to make a huge difference.

King Hezekiah was facing the mighty King of Assyria and his vast army. They were threatening him and his people. Fear gripped the whole nation of Judah. Judah was outnumbered—out gunned (so to speak)—and had worse equipment and fewer horses than Assyria. In fact, looking at the situation from their human eyes, they were in pretty bad shape. So what does the leader (King Hezekiah) of the people do? He goes to church, to "the temple of the Lord." What does he do while he's there? He prays. My friend, you may think that going to church and praying doesn't do anything, but (believe me) it does.

As I said a moment ago, yes, you can pray wherever you are but when you have the chance, when you can, go to God's house. Go to his temple and PRAY. What were the results of Hezekiah's going to the temple of the Lord to pray? Well, let me share it with you. "That night the angel of the Lord went out to the Assyrian camp and killed 185,000 Assyrian troops ... then King Sennacherib of Assyria broke camp and returned to his own land. He went home." You decide, did it make a difference when King Hezekiah went to the temple—to church—and prayed? I would submit that it made all the difference in the world. Try it!

God bless!

Unmet Needs

Scripture: *"When the poor and needy search for water and there is none, and their tongues are parched from thirst, then I, the Lord, will answer them.... Everyone will see this miracle and understand that it is the Lord, the Holy One of Israel, who did it."*
(Isaiah 41:17-20 NLT)

DEVOTIONAL

There are times when things have happened to me and I knew, beyond a shadow of doubt, that it was God who did it. God has a way of doing things that lets us know that nothing is impossible for Him. We sometimes take credit for God's work. Other people say things like "you were very lucky." But to be honest, "luck" doesn't exist in God's vocabulary. God knows exactly what he's doing and He knows exactly what you and I need.

I can recall times when it seemed like all hope was gone and my enemies would prevail. But just when my enemies (and to be honest, I, too) thought that they had won, God stepped in and did what can only be called "a miracle." He did it in such a way that I knew it, my enemies knew it, and everyone else knew that this deliverance came ONLY from God. This is one reason the reading for today was so meaningful to me. God said through his prophet "when the poor and needy search for water and there is none...then I, the Lord will answer them." God assured his people that, whatever their needs, He would "never forsake them," and He would provide for them. As you prepare for Thanksgiving, remember the words of our Lord: "I will answer them ... and will never forsake them." God will fill your tables with food, fill your heart with his love, and fill your mind with his spirit.

God bless!

"I can understand why God said David was 'a man after my own heart.'"

Thanks

Scripture: *"I will give You thanks with all my heart; I will sing Your praise before the heavenly beings."*

(Psalm 138 HCSB)

DEVOTIONAL

David had a beautiful way of putting things when it came to expressing how he felt about God. I have been an admirer of David for a long time, particularly of his relationship with God. The more I read about his life, the more I can understand why God said David was "a man after My own heart." When I first read that statement and realized what God had said about one of his own, I made up in my mind that I, too, wanted to be one after God's own heart. I developed the practice of "praise" that I think David had. David praised God for everything! He praised Him for deliverance! He praised Him for life! He praised Him for victories! He was a "praising" individual and because he was, I think he had a joy filled life. I wanted to be a "praising' individual also, and therefore I decided to develop the art of "praising" God regardless of what was going on around me or what was going on in my life. I discovered that the more I praised God, the more at peace I became. Equally, I tried to be more "thankful" and to thank God more for the things that He has done and to complain less about the things that bothered me. The results were the same. I found myself more joyful and at peace! Listen to the words of David: "I will give You thanks with all my heart; I will sing Your praise before the heavenly beings. I will bow down toward Your holy temple and give thanks to Your name for Your constant love and faithfulness."

God bless!

"Do not be afraid,
for I have ransomed you."

Ransom

Scripture: *"But now, O Israel, the Lord who created you says: Do not be afraid, for I have ransomed you. I have called you by name: you are mine. When you go through deep waters and great trouble, I will be with you."*

(Isaiah 43:1-3 NLT)

DEVOTIONAL

God knows exactly the right scripture to bring to you when you need it most. This is particularly true for me at this moment, because in a day or two I have a very stressful but important meeting. I have to face one who is not kind but mean-spirited, and who has said some harsh things. Yes, initially, anger surfaced and fear attempted to overpower me, but (as He so often does) God spoke to my heart with these words of comfort: "Do not be afraid, for I have ransomed you." Ransomed me? Wow, God said to me, little ole me, that I have been ransomed.

The picture here is beautiful! It's a picture of you (or me) being kidnapped and your captor (or captors) demanding a payment for your release. When the phone rings, God answers the phone and says to your captor(s), "How much will it take for you to release him (or her)?" Then, without question, he pays the ransom price and you are set free. Why would God do that? Well, the answer is clear! He would do it because "I have called you by name; you are mine." You see, my brothers and sisters, when you have been called by God ... when God knows your name ... when you belong to God ... there is no reason to "fear." Now you may ask, "Why shouldn't I fear?" and I'm glad you asked. So let me restate once again why you should not fear and let me answer your question. You don't have to fear because of the assurance that God has given, and it's a very powerful assurance. When we go through "deep waters and great troubles," He has promised that He would be "with" us. Still not convinced that you shouldn't have fear or be fearful? Give me a call and I'll pray with you!

God bless!

Chaplain King overlooks Rio de Janerio, Brazil.

The Potter

Scripture: *"Does a clay pot ever argue with its maker? Does the clay dispute with the one who shapes it, saying,' Stop, you are doing it wrong!' Does the pot exclaim, 'how clumsy can you be!'"*
(Isaiah 45:9-10 NLT)

DEVOTIONAL

I laughed when I read this scripture. Picture this, a potter is making a clay bowl and the bowl starts talking to the maker (the potter), saying, "Stop, you are making me wrong. You are doing it the wrong way... that's not how I want to look or to be made." Sound strange? You bet it does! It's strange because the maker of the bowl has every right to make it just the way he/she wants. The maker knows how he wants the bowl to look. The maker knows what colors he wants the bowl to be, and how large, small, wide, and deep he wants it. The bowl has no right WHATSOEVER to tell the maker what to do. The bowl didn't purchase the materials for itself to be made. The potter did. The potter did it with his own money, and therefore, he has every right to determine just how he wants the bowl to look. You get it?

God is our maker! God is the potter! We are the clay! He created us in his own image, made us out of the material that He purchased (the dust from the earth ... by the way, that He made), and bought us with his own blood. He shapes us, molds us, and makes us into the beings that He wants us to be. Believe me, our potter knows what he's doing. He guides our footsteps and He determines what direction He wants us to go. That's why He said through his servant that the steps of a good man/woman are ordered by the Lord (the potter). The problem is not with the "potter," the problem is with the "clay" (you and me). The potter knows exactly what he's doing with you and me, and He does his job very well.

God bless!

"They all come together for the one
purpose: "Winning the battle."

One Goal

Scripture: *"Under his direction, the whole body is fitted together perfectly. As each part does its own special work, it helps the other parts grow, so that the whole body is healthy and growing and full of love."*

(Ephesians 4:16 NLT)

DEVOTIONAL

The military has taught me many things. I have watched over the years how all the various groups come together in order to win a battle. All branches (Marines, Navy, Army, Air Force, Coast Guard) have their own identities, their own philosophies, their own battle cries. However, when it comes to fighting a battle, they all come together for the one purpose: "Winning the battle" and "defeating the enemy." Yes, there are differences among all of them! Yes, there are times when all of them discuss the issue of who is the toughest and the greatest. But when all is said and done, when all of them hit the battlefield, they are united under the banner of Old Glory. The one thread that brings them all together is the knowledge that "togetherness" is the best and only way to defeat the enemy and win the war. We, as Christians, should have the same philosophy.

We have many body parts but one body. Paul said to the Ephesians, "the whole body is fitted together perfectly. As each part does its own special work, it helps the other parts grow, so that the whole body is healthy and growing and full of love." Notice Paul's words: "each body part is fitted together perfectly." When we function together as "one body" in Christ, we fit together and function together perfectly. When we function together perfectly, we help one another to grow, to stay healthy, and to express love. The problem comes when one part of the body goes off selfishly and tries to accomplish a task or job alone, without the help of the other body parts. You see, my friends, God fixed it so that we can't be successful without one another. I need you. You need me. We need each other. It's like the song writer said, "I need you, you need me, we're all a part of God's body; stay with me, agree with me, we're all a part of God's body." Let's try to function as one! Are you willing to try?

God bless!

Discipline

Scripture: *"For I was angry with My chosen people and began their punishment by letting them fall into your hands. But you, Babylon, showed them no mercy."*

(Isaiah 47:6-7, 11 NLT)

DEVOTIONAL

If I wasn't convinced before reading Isaiah 47, I am convinced now that God will use your enemy to get you in line. Reflecting on my life, I can honestly remember times when God allowed me to be disciplined by and/or through an enemy. Like Israel, those times were usually when I was disobedient or out of the will of God and trying to do things my way. (Yes, it is true, I have to be disciplined by God at times.)

Why would God do this? He would and will discipline you because He loves you and wants nothing but the best for you and for your life. The scripture says, "Those whom God loves He discipline." When God is disciplining you, there are only two things for you to do: (1) repent and (2) go through the discipline with the knowledge that because He (God) loves you, He will watch over you as you are being disciplined. The other thing that I noticed about Israel's being punished or disciplined by her enemy is that God did not approve of the attitude of the enemy.

In fact He specifically said to the enemy (Babylon), "I was angry with My chosen people and began their punishment by LETTING (all caps by me) them fall into your hands. But, you, Babylon, showed them no mercy." God was not pleased that Babylon did not show his "chosen people" mercy and "forced even the elderly to carry heavy burdens." Think about it! God expects one's enemy to "show mercy" to "his chosen." Sound confusing? Let me clarify! The scripture says, be good unto all men especially those that are of the household of faith. Yes, we are to love our enemy. Yes, we are to pray for those who despitefully use us, but we are to pay special attention to those who are the "chosen people" of God.

When Babylon failed to show mercy to God's chosen people, this is what God said would happen: "Disaster will overtake you suddenly, and you won't be able to charm it away. Calamity will fall upon you, and you won't be able to buy your way out. A catastrophe will arise so fast that you won't know what hit you." Listen up, the bottom line is that God requires showing mercy to all, but especially to "the chosen people of God."

God bless!

Comfort

Scripture: *"Comfort, comfort My people, says your God. Speak tenderly to Jerusalem, and announce to her that her time of servitude is over, her iniquity has been pardoned, and she has received from the Lord's hand double for all her sins."*

(Isaiah 40:1-2 HCSB)

DEVOTIONAL

It is a beautiful thing when you come out of a time of testing, trial, tribulation, and punishment. I don't know about you, but I breathe a sigh of relief and spend much time thanking God for seeing me through. I'm sure the people of God were just as glad when they received these encouraging words from the prophet Isaiah: "Comfort, comfort My people, says your God. Speak tenderly to Jerusalem, and announce to her that her time of servitude is over." The people of God were going through a difficult time due to their disobedience to God, and as a result they were being disciplined. Life was pretty rough. But in today's scripture reading, God is announcing through the prophet Isaiah that their time of suffering is about to be over and come to an end. As I have said before, God does discipline, but He forgives, restores and comforts us once we repent and get right with Him. God doesn't enjoy disciplining and/or punishing us, but He does it because of our stubbornness and our disobedience. Also, He loves us and wants the best for us. Make no mistake about it, God wants to bless you beyond your wildest imagination and all He wants in return is for you to give Him the praise, give Him the honor, and love Him with your whole heart, soul, mind and strength. Maybe you have been going through something and wondering when will it all end? Well, I have good news for you. It is ending now. I can say this because I am your Isaiah and I come to say to you as the prophet Isaiah said to the people of his day, "your time of servitude is over." Be encouraged today and receive the blessing that God has for you.

God bless!

Private Matters

Scripture*: "My hair has never been cut, because I am a Nazirite to God from birth. If I am shaved, my strength will leave me, and I will become weak and be like any other man."*

(Judges 16:17 NLT)

Devotional

There are some things that you should not share with anyone. God does not mean for you to tell everything that He tells you. You must remember that some conversations between you and God are meant for just that: to stay between you and God. We make the mistake of believing that our relatives, friends, co-workers, Christians, pastors, etcetera, should know everything that God has told us and that they have our best interests at heart.

The truth, however, is that not all family members, friends, mean us good. So many of us have been discouraged because we have shared what we were not supposed to share. Some of us have doubted God's promise, doubted God's word, and doubted God's assurance simply because we shared a conversation that took place between us and God when we should have kept our mouth closed. Reflect for a moment when you heard a word, a promise, or an assurance from God and then shared it with someone only to hear that person say, "I wouldn't do that if I were you." Samson was told the source of his strength, no doubt, by his parents. His parents did their job! They told him what God had told them, and Samson knew that he was not supposed to reveal where his strength came from. Instead of doing the right thing and instead of keeping his mouth closed and not revealing what God had directed, he spilled the beans (so to speak) and told the lady of his life the secret of his strength.

A lesson for you and me is this, when God reveals something to you, be sure that it is okay for you to reveal it to someone else. If not, KEEP IT TO YOURSELF!

God bless!

"Okay, why am I laughing now?"

Laughter

Scripture: *"Listen to me, you who know right from wrong and cherish My law in your hearts. Do not be afraid of people's scorn or their slanderous talk. For the moth will destroy them as it destroys clothing. The worm will eat away at them as it eats wool. But My righteousness will last forever. My salvation will continue from generation to generation."*

(Isaiah 51:7-8 NLT)

DEVOTIONAL

God knows how to make me laugh! Has He ever made you laugh? If not ask Him to do so, and it will feel "good "when He does. Okay, why am I laughing now? Well, listen to what the Lord said about my/your enemies and what He will do to them. Are you ready for a laugh? Here we go. God said: "Listen to me, you who know right from wrong and cherish My law in your heart. Do not be afraid of people's scorn or their slanderous talk. For [this is funny—my words] the moth will destroy them as it destroys clothing. The worm will eat away at them as it eats wool." Now, I have to admit that when I read this I laughed so hard that I thought I'd be kicked off the plane in midair (I was flying when I wrote this). I laughed because I said to myself, "Why do I concern myself with lying folks or slanderous people?" To be honest I don't know and I don't know why any of us Christians do. There is no reason to do so, my friends. Go ahead, have yourself a laugh right now—today. Stop what you are doing right now and listen to the word of God and then have yourself a great big laugh. "Do not be afraid of people's scorn or their slanderous talk. For the moth will destroy them as it destroys clothing. The worm will eat away at them as it eats wool. But My righteousness will last forever." Praise the Lord and join me as we say together, "Amen."

God bless!

P.S. Stand by for more laughs and part 2 tomorrow!

Laughter, Part 2

Scripture: *"So why are you afraid of mere humans, who wither like the grass and disappear? Yet you have forgotten the Lord, your Creator, the one who put the stars in the sky and established the earth. Will you remain in constant dread of human oppression? Will you continue to fear the anger of your enemy from morning till night.... For I am the Lord.... And I have put My words in your mouth and hidden you safely within My hand."*

(Isaiah 51:12-16 NLT)

DEVOTIONAL

Okay, are you ready to laugh some more? I hope so because when we read God's word again, we can't help but laugh at how we stress out over trivial things, trivial individuals, and trivial circumstances. I must warn you, however, that today the laugh is on me personally. I found myself feeling joyfully sad. I realize that this sounds strange, because it is. I felt sad after remembering all the times I had given up my joy simply because I focused on my enemies and/or my adversaries. Today's reading makes me think of the song, "What a Friend We Have in Jesus." The hymnist writes, "Oh what peace we often forfeit. Oh what needless pain we bear, all because we do not carry everything to God in prayer." You see, my friends, we get too caught up in the "them." The "them" are those around me, those attacking me, those against me. Why be sad? God is in control of the "them" as well as the "me." So, come on, let's laugh again and let's laugh out loud as we listen to the blessed assurance from God: "My name is the Lord Almighty. And I have put My words in your mouth and HIDDEN YOU SAFELY WITHIN MY HAND" (all caps from me). One last thing, please understand what God has just said: you are "hidden" within the safe hand of God. To be hidden safely within God's hand is to be secure. So I laugh joyfully! Go ahead, have a laugh right now!

God bless!

"...this just might be the time
when God will "show me favor."

Answers

Scripture: *"But I keep right on praying to you, Lord, hoping this is the time you will show me favor. In your unfailing love, O God, answer my prayer with your sure salvation."*

(Psalm 69:1-18 NLT)

DEVOTIONAL

If you think that you are the only one having problems, read all of Psalm 69. Here is a person who is crying out to God for help. He seems to be feeling overwhelmed by the pressures of life: he's exhausted emotionally and mentally; his enemies are numerous; he is hated by many; he is talked about, made fun of, and is "the favorite topic of town gossip, and [even, my word] all the drunkards sing about Him."

This person is dealing with the throes of life. But I like how he handles the situation. We, too, can take a lesson from the psalmist regarding how he handles the pressures of life. He (the psalmist) turns to the only person who can set him free and bring him relief: the Lord. The psalmist prays to God to help him: "I keep on praying to you, Lord, hoping this is the time you will show me favor." His statement implies that this is not the first time that he has asked God for help. It implies that indeed he has asked previously, but he will not stop asking and/or praying because this just might be the time when God will "show me favor."

Have you ever felt like that? I have. You, too, have probably felt like the psalmist and, let me warn you, you will feel this way again. Our adversary (the devil/Satan) will not stop and he wants us to "quit" and to stop praying. My friends don't do it. Keep praying. Keep praying until heaven stops what it is doing and tends to your cry! Keep praying until the angels of God sound the trumpet of freedom! Keep praying until God Almighty hears your prayer, wipes away your tears, and delivers you from bondage. A constant and continuous prayer life will heal your body, mend your broken heart and spirit, and bring joy to your life daily.

God bless!

Past

Scripture: *"Put Babylon behind you, with everything it represents, for it is unclean to you. You are the Lord's holy people. Purify yourselves, you who carry home the vessels of the Lord. You will not leave in a hurry, running for your lives. For the Lord will go ahead of you, and the God of Israel will protect you from behind."*

(Isaiah 52:11-12 NLT)

DEVOTIONAL

Leave your past behind! So many people are plagued by their past. They live in the past in their own mind, and they allow others to keep them in the past by constantly bringing up the past. Don't do that or allow that to be done to you, my friends. Always remember that when God forgives, He forgives fully. When God forgives, it is done, complete, and has been put under the blood of Jesus NEVER to rise again ... unless, of course, you or someone else brings it up. Don't allow your past or anyone dredging up your past to cause you grief when God has already put your past behind you. If God puts your past behind you, why won't and shouldn't you do the same? The Lord said through the prophet Isaiah to his people: "Put Babylon [your past, my words] behind you, with everything it represents, for it is unclean to you. You are the Lord's holy people."

I must warn you, however, that in order to put your past behind you, there must be a change in your present. You can't continue to do the same things and hang out with the same people who are doing the same things and expect to leave your past behind. Once God delivers you from a past full of hurt, anger, resentment, bad things, unhealthy people, and things that have plagued you for years, you must make a change and that may mean changing your environment, changing the people you hang out with, and changing your friends. Some people won't like you for changing! Some will call you "stuck up" or "snooty" or many other things, but it doesn't matter because (remember) "You are the Lord's holy people ... and the God of Israel will protect you."

So, my friends, you can leave your past behind by constantly keeping your eyes looking forward and looking to God who is the author and perfecter of your faith.

God bless!

Love

Scripture: *"Live a life filled with love for others, following the example of Christ, who loved you and gave Himself as a sacrifice to take away your sins. And God was pleased, because that sacrifice was like sweet perfume to Him."*

(Ephesians 5:2 NLT)

DEVOTIONAL

As we prepare for Christ's birthday, let us think about what Paul admonished us to do: "Live a life filled with love for others." After all, Christmas is all about love: love for God, love for one another, love for country, love for enemies, love for neighbors, love for your chaplain (smile). It's all about love. Let us "follow the example of Christ" during this time of love season. Let us have a "sacrificial love," the kind of love that Christ had for you and me. It is a love that causes us to think of others first and to sacrifice the "me" attitude for the "you" attitude. It is a love that's less about a present under a tree, but more about a Savior that hung on a tree. It is a love that's more about giving than receiving. You see, my friends, Christmas is about giving. It's about God giving us Christ (his only Son) to take our place on the cross in order that we may live and not have to die. Christmas is about new birth, not only Christ's birth, but our birth. Christmas is about a new outlook—a new outlook on life, a new outlook toward one another, and a new outlook toward self. Christmas is about "God being pleased" because the Son that was born (his Son) was the perfect sacrifice and that perfect sacrifice (his Son) was "like sweet perfume to Him [God]." Do you want to be sweet perfume to God? Then do what Paul recommends and God requires: "Live a life filled with love for others."

God bless!

"Keep Hope Alive."

Hope

Scripture*: "For the mountains may depart and the hills disappear, but even then I will remain loyal to you. My covenant of blessing will never be broken, says the Lord, who has mercy on you."*
(Isaiah 54:10 NLT)

DEVOTIONAL

There are many ways that Satan will attack you, but there is one thing that he wants you to lose—hope. When all hope is gone, when you no longer can feel hopeful, when you have allowed yourself to sink down to the level of being a hopeless individual, you are headed down a path that will lead to destruction and Satan knows that. The Rev. Jessie Jackson, during his campaign for president, coined the phrase "Keep Hope Alive." He was encouraging all to never lose hope!

The Bible said the same thing long ago: "Now faith is the substance of things hoped for and the evidence of things not seen." If we want to live a joyous life, we must hold on to hope. Your question may be, "How can I do that?" Always realize it is a matter of "when," not "if." The question should never be, "*if* God delivers me," but the statement must always be, "*when* God delivers me." The word "if" implies uncertainty, but the word "when" speaks in the affirmative. "If" implies doubt; "when" implies hope. Job, during the most difficult time of his life, said, "I will wait until my change comes." He knew that his change was going to come. He didn't know exactly when, but he knew that it was going to happen.

I can't promise you that dark days will not come upon you. In fact, I can promise you that they will. However, by the same token, I can promise you that if you keep hope alive, your midnight will be turned into day. Why or how can I make this promise? God made it first, and He made it to you. Listen to his promise: "For the mountains may depart and the hills disappear, but even then I will remain LOYAL [caps from me] to you. My covenant of blessing will never be broken, says the Lord, who has mercy on you." My friends, that's a promise that you can not only '"hope" in but "believe" in. Keep hope alive!

God bless!

Light

Scripture: *"Arise, Jerusalem! Let your light shine for all the nations to see! For the glory of the Lord is shining upon you."*
(Isaiah 60:1 NLT)

DEVOTIONAL

Today's scripture reading reminds me of what Jesus said to all of us. Jesus' words were very similar to what God said through the prophet Isaiah: "Let your light so shine before men that they may see your good works and glorify the Father in heaven." It is amazing how both the Old and New Testaments state clearly that we as people of God are supposed to be the light of the world. The words we speak, the way we act, our behavior, our attitude, our way of life are supposed to be about "letting our light shine for all the nations to see." It may be difficult to do at times, but by the power of the Holy Spirit, we can let our light shine at all times. Remember that God has placed his light of happiness, his light of joy, his light of hope within you and the godly light that is within you may be the only light that people will see. Let the light of God shine through you!

God bless!

Chaplain King and local church leaders in Tanzania.

Unfinished Work

Scripture: *"And I am sure that God, who began the good work within you, will continue his work until it is finally finished on that day when Christ Jesus comes back again."*

(Philippians 1:6 NLT)

DEVOTIONAL

James Cleveland wrote a song with these lyrics: "please be patient with me, God is not through with me yet. When God gets through with me, I shall come forth as pure gold." Paul's words confirm what Mr. Cleveland was singing about. God is not finished with any of us yet. We may make mistakes; we may get off track and go down the wrong path; we may even violate God's word, but when we are saved by his (God's) grace, He has begun a "good work within" us that will not be complete until Christ comes back again. Notice what Paul said, "God, who began the good work within you." To begin means that the work is not complete.

We should be careful not to write ourselves or others off so quickly. We make the mistake of seeing an individual or ourselves the way we are now and give up, not realizing, or holding on to the fact, that God is not finished with us and the work that He started is not done.

As Mr. Cleveland writes, "please be patient with me." He is correct, but we, too, must be patient with ourselves. The work that God started with each of us is a life-long process and it will not be complete until the Master (Jesus) comes back to receive us unto Himself. The fact that we celebrate Christ's birthday says that God didn't write us off as human beings. Had He written us off, He would not have sent his "only"

Son (Jesus) on Christmas morning. My friends, I too, encourage you with the words of Paul as my own words to you: "I am sure that God, who began the good work within you, will continue his work until it is finally finished on that day when Christ Jesus comes back again." If God is patient with you, so shall I be also! Will you do the same toward one another?

God bless!

Perfect Gift

Scripture: *"No longer will you need the sun or moon to give you light, for the Lord your God will be your everlasting light, and He will be your glory. The sun will never set, the moon will not go down. For the Lord will be your everlasting light."*

(Isaiah 60:19-20 NLT)

DEVOTIONAL

There will come a time when we, as children of God, will no longer need the sun or the moon, but our light will come totally from God's Son, Christ Jesus. No more gas or electric bills, no more worrying about winter or summer, no more winter or summer clothes, no more concern about high gas prices and no more worry about anything because God "will be our everlasting light and He will be our glory." All of this is possible because Christ (God's Son) is the true reason for the season. Because Christ is the true reason for the season, we can lie in hope and expectation of the following: "Peace and righteousness will be our leaders! Violence will disappear from our land; the desolation and destruction of war will end. Salvation will surround us like city walls, and praise will be on the lips of all." When that baby boy (Jesus) was born on Christmas morning, He gave us more than a Christmas tree or presents under the tree. He gave us something to look forward to that had been lost in the Garden of Eden ... a chance to be with the Father in heaven. On Christmas morning Christ gave us the best gift of all: Himself! So as we continue to prepare for his birth, let us, too, be thankful and appreciative by giving ourselves to Him.

God bless!

"How do you see trials and tribulation?"

Trials

Scripture: *"And I want you to know, dear brothers and sisters, that everything that has happened to me here has helped to spread the Good News."*

(Philippians 1:12-14 NLT)

DEVOTIONAL

I have three questions to ask you. One, how do you see trials and tribulation? Two, do you see them as a setback, a stumbling block, or a stepping stone? Three, do you see them as opportunities or curses? You see, my friends, how we view tribulation and things that happen to us makes all the difference in the world when it comes to our sanity and our peace of mind. Paul's words make it obvious that he did not see tribulation as a stumbling block, a curse, a hindrance, or a setback. How did Paul see tribulation? Well, let's see, according to his own words: "I want you to know... that everything that has happened to me here has helped to spread the Good News." Paul was in "chains" and in "prison" when he wrote these words. Yet, he confessed that his chains and imprisonment served as an opportunity "to spread the Good News" about Christ. Christ, before Paul, saw tribulation in the same manner. When Christ was born on Christmas Day, He knew the future held death on a cross. Yet He did it, and He did it because of the love that He had for you and me. Christ knew that what faced Him after Christmas Day was a future of teaching, preaching, healing, and ultimately a cross. He saw this as an opportunity to "spread the Good news" and to bring all of us back into a right relationship with God the Father. Your tribulations and trials, your challenges and struggles, and your ups and downs, are just opportunities for you to realize that everything that has and is happening to you is an opportunity to share the Good News of God. Go out, my brothers and sisters, and tell the Good News that a Savior was born, and since then we have been singing "Joy to the World, the Lord Is Come."

God bless!

"Listen to the words of the angel:
'a Savior was born for you.'"

Good News

Scripture: *"Don't be afraid, for look, I proclaim to you good news of great joy that will be for all the people; today a Savior, who is Messiah the Lord, was born to you."*

(Luke 2:10-12 NLT)

DEVOTIONAL

The birth of Jesus was not just for one group of people but it was for "all the people." There is no other day or celebration that is as highly celebrated as the birth of Jesus, especially in America. Almost all over the globe, almost in every part of the world, but definitely in America, December 25 is set aside as "Christmas," which represents the birth of a Savior. Many may not acknowledge Him as Savior, but there are very few, if any, who do not celebrate his birthday. In recent years, there has been much talk about whether or not it is appropriate to say "Merry Christmas," and many of us Christians have bought into the senseless argument. As a result, we too, on many occasions, will respond with "happy holidays" instead of "Merry Christmas."

December 25 always has been marked on our calendars as "Christmas" and "Christmas" has always been about the birth of a Savior (Jesus). To make it about anything else or to be afraid to say what it really is and what it really means is not only a shame, but borders on being sinful. When the shepherds received the good news from the angel, they were told, "don't be afraid" for "today a Savior was born for you." Listen to the words of the angel: "a Savior was born for you." If a Savior is born for someone, why wouldn't that person want to tell the world the good news? Well, we, too, should not be afraid of telling the good news that a Savior has been born for us, for you and "for all the people." That's a good news story that's worth telling, and we should tell it on top of the mountain, in the lowest part of the valley, and on every street corner. The world already knows that we Christians are occasionally afraid to say, "Merry Christmas." The world already knows that we Christians celebrate the 25th as Christmas and that Christmas is about Christ, so why are we Christians afraid to say what the world already knows? December 25 means "Merry Christmas." Think about it!

God bless!

Depression

Scripture*: "I am torn between two desires: Sometimes I want to live, and sometimes I long to go and be with Christ. That would be far better for me, but it is better for you that I live."*

(Philippians 1:23 NLT)

DEVOTIONAL

Everybody gets down at one time or another regardless of how strong he or she is or how much the person goes to church. Please do not think that you are in this struggle alone, because you are not. In fact, I would say that you are in some pretty good company. You are in the company of giants. One such giant was the apostle Paul, who was a strong Christian man, one who loved the Lord, one who wrote more epistles than anybody else, one who was bold in his faith, one who maintained his commitment and his walk with Christ. Yet, listen to what he said, "I'm torn between two desires: Sometimes I want to live, and sometimes I long to go and be with Christ. That would be far better for me."

My friends, God wants you to remember that to get down is not a sin nor is it unnatural. It is very human and natural to do so. However, here is what you have to be watchful about and to be aware of—that you don't allow yourself to stay down. There are many things that God will show you in order to keep you encouraged and to keep you from "staying down." For example, one reason Paul leaned toward being in this life and not with the Lord immediately was because of those to Whom he ministered and Whom he loved. The Philippian church was Paul's baby (if you will), and he loved each and every one of them dearly. He said, "I long to go and be with Christ. That would be far better for me, but it is better for you that I live." Paul knew that God was using him to bless others, and for that he leaned toward his second desire—"to live for his flock." Please remember that you, too, have many people who are blessed by your presence, your encouragement, and your life. I encourage you to be a part of other people's lives. The next time you are feeling down, stop and think that there are those of us out here who are blessed because of you. You are valuable. You are special. You are appreciated. You are loved. I join Paul in saying "Sometimes I want to live, sometimes I long to go and be with Christ ... but it is better for you that I live" because my life is enriched by yours. When I think about the lives that God uses me to touch and how so many of you touch and enrich my life, my "down-ness" leaves me immediately. Thank you. Christians such as you keep Christians like me going!

God bless!

Resolution

Scripture: *"I will answer them before they even call to Me. While they are still talking to Me about their needs, I will go ahead and answer their prayers ... I, the Lord, have spoken!"*

(Isaiah 65:24-25 NLT)

DEVOTIONAL

I will memorize, recite, and meditate on Isaiah 65:24-25 for an entire year. Read it again and tell me that it is not worth meditating on for one full year. "I will answer them BEFORE [caps mine] they even call to me. While they are still talking to me about their needs, I will go ahead and answer their prayers!" Wow! What a wonderful thought. To KNOW, not just to realize, but to KNOW that even before you ask, even before you call upon our heavenly Father, He has said, "I will answer them."

Translated, I will answer you, even before you call upon my name and ask me for what you need. Now, this is a good time to feel some New Year's "goose bumps" (remember them?). Think about it, my friends. God said while you are praying about how you are going to make it in and/or through, while you are praying about the economy, while you are praying about the rising cost of living, while you are praying about all of your needs, God has already said, "I will go ahead and answer their prayers!" The only things that God wants you to do are (1) to talk to Him—in other words, "pray;" and (2) to trust Him. He has assured you and me that (let me say it again), "I will answer them before they even call to me. While they are still talking to me about their needs [while they are still on their knees or in a state of reverence, praying], I will go ahead and answer their prayers... I, the Lord have spoken!"

God bless!

"…rain on the unjust
as well as the just."

Envy

Scripture: *"Truly God is good to Israel, to those whose hearts are pure. But as for me, I came so close to the edge of the cliff! My feet were slipping, and I was almost gone. For I envied the proud when I saw them prosper despite their wickedness."*

(Psalm 73:1-28 NLT)

Devotional

When looking at the wealth and success of others, do you ever ask the question, "How can they get all this without serving God?" If you think there is no danger in that question, I ask you to read Psalm 73 in its entirety. There are many questions that we can't answer. One of those is why do the unrighteous prosper and in many instances the righteous seem not to prosper? When asking this question, however, please keep in mind what the Bible says. God allows it to rain on the unjust as well as the just. We have to be careful that we do not focus so much on what others have that we find ourselves in the shoes of the psalmist: "I came so close to the edge of the cliff! My feet were slipping and I was almost gone. For I envied the proud when I saw them prosper despite their wickedness." When we look too much at others, and what others are getting out of life, we run the risk of thinking that there is no reason to serve God, and our service to God becomes "for nothing." If, my brothers and sisters, we find ourselves in this state of mind, we are close to the cliff. We are saying with the psalmist, "All I get is trouble all day long; every morning brings me pain." Some have lived their entire life with the bitter pain of thinking that God has wronged them, is not fair to them, and has been better to the wicked (or to others) than to them. If you are in this situation now, or if you find yourself slipping into this mindset, here's what you need

157

to do to get out of it.

Recognize that this has happened to you and be honest about it. If you are jealous of others and what they are or have accomplished, admit it. Confess to God that you feel this way and repent. The first step to being healed of a problem such as this is to be honest about how you feel and to repent.

The third thing to do is to say the words of the psalmist out loud, "I still belong to you; you are holding my right hand. You will keep on guiding me with your counsel, leading me to a GLORIOUS [all caps my idea] destiny."

Remember, when God leads, He leads you in and down the path of righteousness for his namesake. Your destiny is in God's hand, and what better hands could your destiny or you be in? Don't forget, read all of Psalm 73!

God bless!

Rebuke

Scripture: *"Man must not live on bread alone, but on every word that comes from the mouth of God.... Do not test the Lord your God.... Go away, Satan."*

(Matthew 4:1-11 HCSB)

DEVOTIONAL

Matthew 4:1-11 is an excellent example of how best to combat Satan's attacks. Jesus gives us the perfect way to defeat Satan as well as to recognize him for who he is and what he stands for. Using the method that Jesus used, I want to give you three ways to defeat Satan. I'm convinced that this method will work every time.

(1) When God gives you a gift, power, or confirmation, don't try to prove that you have the gift or the ability to do a certain thing. Satan said to Jesus, "If you are the Son of God do such and such." In other words, prove that you are who you say that you are. Jesus could have proved that He indeed was the Son of God, but why should He have bothered trying to prove it to a "devil"? When you know who you are, whose you are, and what you are called to do, don't try to prove the truth to anyone.

(2) Know the scriptures for yourself so that if someone quotes a scripture or verse to you, you will know if it is being taken out of context. Remember, the devil reads and knows scripture and will use it to get you off balance. Every scripture that is quoted to you may not be for you or apply to you or your situation at that time. Satan quoted scripture to Jesus but Jesus knew that He was taking that scripture out of context, and the Lord did what we, too,

should do in that instance. We should respond with these words of scripture: "Do not test the Lord your God." In other words, do not use scripture for your own selfish reasons or to try to tempt me!

(3) Don't continue to stand for the attacks or prompting of Satan. Get in the habit of doing what Jesus did, saying out loud to your tempter, "Go away Satan" or my favorite, "I rebuke you in the name of Jesus." When you speak in the affirmative ("Do not test me. Go away. I rebuke you!"), Satan will leave you alone. Now, he will not leave you alone permanently, but he will leave you alone for the moment.

But here's the deal. Remember that you do not have a limit on the number of times that you can exercise your authority to say to Satan, "Do not test me ... Go away ... I rebuke you." God has given you permission to use all three forever. I'm convinced that the principles that Jesus used when He was in the wilderness of temptation will work for us as well. Remember Jesus' words, "These things shall you do and greater."

God bless!

Courage

Scripture: *"Get up and get dressed. Go out, and tell them whatever I tell you to say. Do not be afraid of them, or I will make you look foolish in front of them. For see, today I have made you immune to their attacks... None of the kings, officials, priests, or people of Judah will be able to stand against you. They will try, but they will fail. For I am with you and I will take care of you."*

(Jeremiah 1:17-19 NLT)

DEVOTIONAL

I don't know about you, but I hate looking foolish in front of anyone. I can recall times when I have been so embarrassed because of something that someone said to me or because of something that I said that made me look totally stupid. It wasn't a good feeling! When God instructs us to do something, He means for us to do it. Not following instructions could mean trouble for us. For Jeremiah, it meant looking foolish in front of his colleagues, associates, enemies, and all those listening. God instructs Jeremiah to tell the people whatever God tells him and not to "be afraid of them." God doesn't tell Jeremiah just to speak, God says to speak what He tells him and not to be afraid of what the people would think, say, feel, or do. He wants Jeremiah to be fearless when he stands up to speak for God. Guess what? He wants us to be the same way, fearless. When we look at the power of God and the assurance that He has given us, we can do exactly that, "be fearless." God said to Jeremiah say what I tell you and remember this "none of the kings, officials, priests, or people ... will be able to stand against you. They will try, but they will fail." Now this is what you call blessed assurance and a remedy for being fearful. The next time you are feeling overwhelmed, fearful or a little scared, remember this. "They will try, but they will fail. For I am with you and I will take care of you." With that kind of support, who needs to be afraid?

God bless!

Chaplain King with Maasai Warriors, who are from a group of people who live along the Kenyan and Tanzanian border.

Carefree

Scripture: *"Don't worry about anything; instead, pray about everything. Tell God what you need, and thank Him for all He has done. If you do this, you will experience God's peace, which is far more wonderful than the human mind can understand. His peace will guard your hearts and minds as you live in Christ Jesus."*

(Philippians 4:6-7)

DEVOTIONAL

How could one who had experienced so much in life speak of "not worrying about anything?" How could one, such as Paul, come to the point in his life that he could say to us, "Don't worry about anything?" He was beaten many times; he was imprisoned several times; he lived under the threat of death most of the time, if not daily. Paul's life was not a life free from suffering and trials and tribulation. Yet we hear him say, "don't worry about anything." How could this be? Well, the key to Paul's worry free life had to do with his constant prayer life. He said, "pray about everything. Tell God what you need, and thank Him for all He has done." There was nothing that Paul didn't pray about. There was nothing that Paul didn't take to God in prayer. The results of constant prayer, according to Paul, are as follows: "you will experience God's peace, which is far more wonderful than the human mind can understand. His peace will guard your hearts and mind as you live in Christ Jesus." Paul took everything to God through prayer and he experienced God's peace. What worked for Paul will also work for us. The key to making it all work is to do as Paul did and as he recommended: "pray about everything. Tell God what you need, and thank Him for all He has done."

God bless!

"I do not want God to turn
his anger away from my enemies
and toward me."

Revenge

Scripture: *"Do not rejoice when your enemies fall into trouble. Don't be happy when they stumble. For the Lord will be displeased with you and will turn his anger away from them. Do not fret because of evildoers; don't envy the wicked. For the evil have no future; their light will be snuffed out."*

(Proverbs 24:17-20 NLT)

DEVOTIONAL

I must admit that this is a tough scripture for me to practice. I have the temptation to say, "Get 'em, Lord," and even a greater temptation for me is to rejoice when God does just that: "Gets 'em!" Proverbs 24:17-20 helps to keep me on track, because I do not want God to turn his anger away from my enemies and toward me. Be cautious, my brothers and sisters, that you do not fall into the temptation of rejoicing when your enemies are being disciplined or punished by God. He doesn't like that! Instead of rejoicing, I recommend that you be watchful, be prayerful, and be vigilant when it comes to how you treat and respond to your enemies. God will deal with your enemies (no doubt about it), but you and I need to pray for them (no doubt about that, too). God will punish your enemies (no doubt about it), but you and I should feed them (no doubt about that, too). God will wipe out your enemies' future (no doubt about it), but you and I are to love our enemies (no doubt about that, too). God will make your enemies your footstool (no doubt about it), but you and I must do good unto those who spitefully use us and say all matter of evil against us (no doubt about that, too). Remember what the writer of Proverbs said God will do to evil: "For the evil have no future; their light will be snuffed out." You and I have to get out of the way and let God do his job. Believe me, he's good at it! God can handle our enemies, but we have to have the right attitude toward them.

"To be chosen by God means that you are special!"

Chosen

Scripture: *"Since God chose you to be the holy people whom He loves, you must clothe yourselves with tenderhearted mercy, kindness, humility, gentleness, and patience."*

(Colossians 3:12 NLT)

DEVOTIONAL

Here's a wonderful thought, "God chose you to be the holy people whom He loves." Think about it! First of all, to be chosen by God is an awesome and wonderful thing. For God to choose us, with all of our shortcomings, is a thought that I want to hold on to for life. Guess what? I recommend that you do the same. The next time you are feeling down and out, shout out in a LOUD voice, "I HAVE BEEN CHOSEN BY GOD!" (Go ahead, try it right now!) If that doesn't make you feel better, nothing will. To be chosen by God means that you are special! To be chosen by God means that no one can un-choose you (I know, bad English, but you get the point). When you realize that the creator of the universe, the Father of all humankind has chosen you to be his very own, what more could you want? What greater honor can one have than to be chosen by God? And guess what? The only thing we have to do to show our appreciation for being chosen is to "clothe ourselves with tenderhearted mercy, kindness, humility, gentleness, and patience." Is that asking too much? I don't think so. It's not asking too much for us to be tenderhearted, kind, merciful, humble, gentle, and patient, is it? The answer is no! Why? It's because God is that way with us. Everyday God shows us his mercy, his grace, his patience, his tender heart, his humility, and his gentleness. If God saw fit to choose us, and we are his, can't we do as He wants us to do by showing his unfailing love toward one another? Think about it! I don't think that is asking too much!

From the sands of Iraq,

God bless!

Chaplain King visits with local school children in Nicaragua.

Love

Scripture: *"And the most important piece of clothing you must wear is love. Love is what binds us all together in perfect harmony."*
(Colossians 3:14 NLT)

DEVOTIONAL

One of the greatest and most powerful words in the Bible is the word "love." Today's scripture reading states that the "most important piece of clothing you must wear is love." The writer didn't say that tenderheartedness, mercy, kindness, humility, gentleness, and patience are not important, because they are. However, he did say that love is the "most" important. Could it be that when we clothe ourselves with true godly love, we will show and express toward one another tenderness, mercy, kindness, humility, gentleness, and patience? I think so! You see my friends, the power of love cannot be under or over stated. It is a powerful weapon to have. It is so powerful that the latter part of verse 14 says, "Love is what binds us ALL [all caps my idea] together in perfect harmony." The meaning here is clear. Where genuine love exists, perfect harmony is revealed.

From the sands of Iraq,

God bless!

"Now, that's what I'm talking about."

Plots

Scripture: *"Then the Lord told me about the plots my enemies were making against me."*

(Jeremiah 11:18 NLT)

DEVOTIONAL

If today's scripture reading does not set your mind at ease about your enemies, nothing will. I have often preached that God will tell you what you need to know, and He will. In today's scripture reading, Jeremiah's enemies were plotting to kill him. Did Jeremiah know of this plot? No! Was Jeremiah aware of a plot against his life? No! But, God knew, and God told him about the plot so that Jeremiah would be aware of what his enemies were planning. He (God) not only informed Jeremiah about the plot, but He also put Jeremiah's mind at ease by assuring him that He would take care of Jeremiah's enemies. (As the young people used to say, "Now that's what I'm talking about.") Remember this, your enemies can make all the plans they like, but God is a "plan destroyer," especially when the plan is to do you harm. Your enemies cannot surprise you! Your enemies have no power or control over you! Your enemies are not in control of you or anything about you. Relax, get some sleep, stop worrying, rejoice, and be at peace. Why? Because God has said, "I will punish them!" You have nothing to worry about!

From the sands of Iraq,

God bless!

"The key is to work for the Lord!"

Cheerfulness

Scripture: *"Work hard and cheerfully at whatever you do, as though you were working for the Lord rather than for people. Remember that the Lord will give you an inheritance as your reward."*

(Colossians 3:23-24 NLT)

DEVOTIONAL

If we follow today's scripture reading to the letter we could save ourselves a lot of heartache. Colossians 3:23-24 gives us a pretty good formula for having a great attitude on any job that we have. The writer says, "Work hard and cheerfully at whatever you do, as though you were working for the Lord rather than for people." The key is to work for the Lord! When we focus on working for the Lord, we focus less on pay raises, promotions, awards, prestige, fame, retirement. Our goal should be to please God and not necessarily our boss. While we may desire our boss's approval, the sole purpose of our work should not be for his/her approval. When we "work hard and cheerfully" (remember the writer said to "work hard and cheerfully"), when we do our best for the Lord, when we work for the evaluation of God, the Lord looks at us when the work is complete and says, WELL DONE! Now, that's a reward that is worth working "hard" and "cheerfully!"

From the sands of Iraq,

God bless!

"We will pay for the wrong we do."

Right and Wrong

Scripture: *"But if you do what is wrong, you will be paid back for the wrong you have done. For God has no favorites who can get away with evil."*

(Colossians 3:25 NLT)

DEVOTIONAL

If I were to give a title to today's "Thought for the Day," I would title it, "An incentive for doing what is right." If there is one scripture that plainly states that we will pay for the wrong we do, it is Colossians 3:25. The writer does not distinguish between a Christian doing wrong and a non-Christian doing wrong. Both Christians and non-Christian must pay for their wrongdoings. We, as Christians, must always be mindful that we do not have a "doing wrong pass" or a "get out of jail free" card just because we are Christians. We have to answer for the things we do, the way we act, and the way we treat one another. The writer says, "For God has no favorites who can get away with evil." If you don't want to pay God for doing wrong, there's one way to avoid it: *don't do wrong.*

From the sands of Iraq,

God bless!

"God wants us to leave 'getting even' to Him."

Adversaries

Scripture: *"Do not testify spitefully against innocent neighbors; don't lie about them. And don't say, 'Now I can pay them back for all their meanness to me! I'll get even.'"*

(Proverbs 24:28-29 NLT)

DEVOTIONAL

Getting even is not a good thing to do. Time and time again I read in the scriptures that God wants us to leave "getting even" to Him, if getting even is to be gotten. Besides, He does a much better job of dealing with our adversaries than we do. We are reminded in today's scripture reading not to testify "spitefully" against our "innocent" neighbors. Be careful, however, that we don't confuse the issue with testifying "spitefully" against a *guilty* neighbor. I'm sure that God is just as displeased when we testify "spitefully" against anyone. The danger of testifying "spitefully" is that we run the risk of trying to "get even" and not leaving things in the hand of God. When we do that, we lose the high ground of allowing God to take care of the situation. Bottom line, if you must testify against a person or neighbor, do so, but just be sure that you are not doing it out of spite.

From the sands of Iraq,

God bless!

Singer/Actress CeCe Winans (center) joins from left, SSG Prosper, SSG Fuller, 1stLt Cavanaugh, Chaplain King and Capt. Hagerty in Uganda.

Nosiness

Scripture: *"This should be your ambition: to live a quiet life, minding your own business and working with your hands, just as we commanded you before. As a result, people who are not Christians will respect the way you live."*

(I Thessalonians 4:11-12 NLT)

DEVOTIONAL

There is a saying that goes like this "you should mind your own business and leave other's business alone." Oh, how much better we would be if we would practice that philosophy. If we could just "stay in our lane" and take care of our own business, we would not have time to meddle in the business and affairs of others. I have counseled so many couples who could have had a great relationship if they had just kept other folks out of their business. I have seen friendships destroyed simply because of other folks meddling into the business of others. In today's scripture reading, we are reminded of the things we should be ambitious about.

We should (1) live a quiet life, (2) mind our own business, and (3) work with our hands.

Powerful stuff, huh? Definitely! Well, if you think that is powerful, listen to the result of doing all three: "people who are not Christians will respect the way you live." Wow! Now, that's what I'm talking about, to live in such a way that "non-Christians" will respect you by the way you live. I want to be that kind of person. What about you?

From the sands of Iraq,

God bless!

"It's not you being rejected, but Christ."

Rejection

Scripture: *"Then He said to the disciples, "Anyone who accepts your message is also accepting Me. And anyone who rejects you is rejecting Me. And anyone who rejects Me is rejecting God who sent Me."*

(Luke 10:16 NLT)

DEVOTIONAL

What a load off the shoulders of the messenger! It is a wonderful thing to realize that you or I don't have to take things personally when someone rejects us for the message that we preach or teach. In fact, God is so good that He says to reject me (the messenger) is to reject Him. Think about it! When we live for Christ, when we let our light shine for Him, when we teach others (by our ways, deeds, actions and words) that we are Christ's messengers, we are free from feeling rejected by others. If you are feeling rejected for your stand for Christ, stop and don't take it personally. It's not you being rejected, but Christ. Keep letting your light shine for Christ. Just make sure that your light is shining for Christ and not for yourself!

From the sands of Iraq,

God bless!

"Christ intercedes on our behalf and says to his Father, 'Be patient' with them."

Patience

Scripture: *"Brothers and sisters, we urge you to warn those who are lazy. Encourage those who are timid. Take tender care of those who are weak. Be patient with everyone."*

(I Thessalonians 5:14 NLT)

DEVOTIONAL

Paul, in today's scripture reading, asks us to do four things as Christians.

1. We are to warn those who are lazy. Now, I am certain that he is not only talking about being lazy on our civilian jobs, but he is also talking about being lazy when comes to God's work. We are to be active Christians for God, working for his purpose and carrying out his plan.

2. We are to encourage those who are timid! We are not to take advantage of, make fun of, or put down those who may not be as strong as we are. Instead, Paul says to "encourage them." Encourage them to keep the faith! Encourage them not to give up! Encourage them to realize that they are special, created in the image and likeness of God.

3. We are to take tender care of those who are weak. Paul didn't just say to take *care* but to "take tender care" of the weak. Wow! This means to be gentle in our caring for those who are weaker than we are. We must remember that all of us are weak in one way or another, and God truly does "take tender care" of us.

4. We are to be patient with everyone. How about that? Paul does not say to "be patient with some" does he? No! He says to be

patient with "everyone."

Even those who get on our last nerve, we must be patient with as well. After all, I'm sure that we, too, try the last nerve of God. But, Christ intercedes on our behalf and says to his Father "Be patient" with them for My sake. And guess what? The Father (God) says, "Okay, I will." We should do exactly the same. Try it!

From the sands of Iraq,

God bless!

Falseness

Scripture: *"But stop using this phrase, 'prophecy from the LORD.' For the people are using it to give authority to their own ideas, turning upside down the words of our God, the living God, the Lord Almighty."*

(Jeremiah 23:36 NLT)

DEVOTIONAL

The prophet Jeremiah's words sound like a warning not only to the people of his day but to those living today as well. We have to be careful that we do not fall for everything that we hear. Just because someone says to us "this prophecy comes from the Lord" or "the Lord told me to say this," doesn't mean that it came from the Lord. We must remember that Jesus cautioned us about false prophets. He told us that in the last days there would be false prophets and that they would be so convincing that they will almost deceive the "very elect." There are a lot of teachers, preachers, prophets, and so forth, out there today and we must be, as Jesus said, "wise as a serpent but harmless as a dove." When you hear someone saying "this prophecy comes from the Lord," check it out. How does one do that? Good question! Ask the Lord! He will tell you. Jeremiah told the prophets and the people to stop using the phrase "prophecy from the Lord" because "they were using it to give authority to their own ideas." Don't fool yourself my brothers and sisters, this is still happening today as well. Be careful; stay prayerful; be vigilant in the word of God and stay so closely connected with the Master (Jesus) that He will keep you from being deceived by false prophets.

From the sands of Iraq,

God bless!

"Don't give up or quit
when things seem
to be going wrong for you."

Perseverance

Scripture: *"Then the Lord said to me, What do you see, Jeremiah? I replied, Figs, some very good and some very bad. Then the Lord gave me this message: This is what the Lord, the God of Israel, says: The good figs represent the exiles I sent from Judah to the land of the Babylonians. I have sent them into captivity for their own good. I will see that they are well treated, and I will bring them back here again. I will build them up and not tear them down."*

(Jeremiah 24:3-7 NLT)

DEVOTIONAL

If you have not been listening to me in the past, please listen to me now. Everything that seems to be bad or going bad in your life is not bad. Don't give up or quit when things seem to be going wrong for you. God has a plan for your life; the plan will be revealed sooner or later and it will be a good plan. God does things that we may not understand at the time they are happening. However, if you continue to trust God, things will work out for your good. In today's scripture reading, God showed Jeremiah two types of figs (one good and one bad). Listen to God's explanation to Jeremiah and take heed to what He is saying to you today: "The good figs represent the exiles ... I have sent them into captivity for their own good." But "I will see that they are well treated, and I will bring them back here again. I will build them up and not tear them down. I will plant them and not uproot them. I will give them hearts that will recognize me as the Lord. They will be My people, and I will be their God." Now, do you see why I made the beginning statement? Whatever is happening in your life, whatever you are going through, however dark your life may be at this moment,

God said through Jeremiah, "I will see that they are well treated ... I will bring them back ... I will build them up and not tear them down ... I will plant them and not uproot them... They will be My people, and I will be their God." This is a promise worth remembering. And all the people said, "Amen!"

From the sands of Iraq,

God bless!

Shouts

Scripture: *"How lovely is your dwelling place, O Lord Almighty. I long, yes, I faint with longing to enter the courts of the Lord. With my whole being, body and soul, I will shout joyfully to the living God."*

(Psalm 84:1-12)

DEVOTIONAL

If you ever feel tired, weary, frustrated and a little down, just stop what you are doing for a moment and read Psalm 84:1-8. Just reading those beautiful words from the psalmist as he describes what it is like when he enters the "courts of the Lord" is uplifting. He talks about the courts of the Lord in such beautiful terms that one (at least for me) can't help but to dream about the beauty of the Lord's courts and lose oneself in thinking about the goodness and greatness of God. If you don't believe me, let me state it for you in its entirety! Right now I want you to relax, read and listen to the word of God. It's going to minister to you now. Here goes:

> How lovely is your dwelling place, O Lord Almighty. I long, yes, I faint with longing to enter the courts of the Lord. With my whole being, body and soul, I will shout joyfully to the living God. [Go ahead shout if you like, my words.] Even the sparrow finds a home there, and the swallow builds her nest and raises her young at a place near your altar; O Lord Almighty, my King and my God! How happy are those who can live in your house, always singing your praises. Happy are those who are strong in the Lord, who set their minds on a pilgrimage to Jerusalem. When they walk through the Valley of Weeping, it will become a place of refreshing springs, where pools of blessing collect after the rains! [This is deep, my comment.] They

will continue to grow stronger; and each of them will appear before God in Jerusalem. O Lord God Almighty, hear my prayer. Listen, O God of Israel. O God, look with favor upon the king, our protector! Have mercy on the one you have anointed. A single day in your courts is better than a thousand anywhere else! I would rather be a gatekeeper in the house of my God than live the good life in the homes of the wicked. For the Lord God is our light and protector. [Praise the Lord, my addition.] He gives us grace and glory. No good thing will the Lord withhold from those who do what is right. O Lord Almighty, happy are those who trust in you.

With a powerful Psalm such as this, the only thing left to say is thank you, LORD!

From the sands of Iraq,

God bless!

God's Call

Scripture: *"So you must submit to Babylon's king and serve him; put your neck under Babylon's yoke! I will punish any nation that refuses to be his slave, says the Lord."*

(Jeremiah 27:8 NLT)

DEVOTIONAL

I have been preaching since 1979. I have preached in many cities, towns, and countries, but never have I had the task of doing what Jeremiah had to do. God directed him to tell the people of God that "you must submit to Babylon's king and serve him." The reason was obvious: SIN. God's people had turned their backs on the one true God, and as a result, God told the prophet Jeremiah to tell them to submit themselves to a Babylon king who would rule over them. Yes, I have had to preach some tough sermons but this, I am sure, was the toughest of all. You talk about feeling alone, sad, and probably a little fearful at times. I'm sure Jeremiah must have felt all of these emotions. Yet, in spite of his aloneness, possible fears, and possible sadness, he obeyed God and preached exactly what God told him to preach. Tough to do, probably! Necessary? Definitely! You see, my friends, when God calls, He doesn't always call us to a pretty task. There are times when He calls us to do fearful things, stand before powerful people, and proclaim a word that will not be accepted by or popular with the masses. But do it. God will see you through. As for Jeremiah, God stood with him, for him, around him, and through him. He will do the same for you!

From the sands of Iraq,

God bless!

"I never understood those words
as a child,
but I think that I have
a better understanding as an adult."

Punishment

Scripture: *"For I am with you and will save you, says the Lord. I will completely destroy the nations where I have scattered you, but I will not destroy you. But I must discipline you; I cannot let you go unpunished."*

(Jeremiah 30:11 NLT)

DEVOTIONAL

When I was growing up, I used to hear some parents say when they were about to discipline their children (and maybe they still do): "This will hurt me more than it hurts you." I'd always think, "Yeah, right." You are not the one getting the belt on your behind (or wherever). I never understood those words as a child, but I think that I have a better understanding as an adult. For you see, I'm sure that it grieved and hurt God to see his beloved children suffer because they failed to listen to his advice and his words. It wasn't, and still isn't, God's desire to see us hurting after He disciplines us. He would much rather see us enjoy the fruits of his labor and experience the joy-filled life that He wants us to have.

However, because of our stubbornness, our selfishness, our determination to do things our way and not his way, we force our heavenly Father to say the words to us that He said to the children of Israel: "For I am with you and will save you ... but I must discipline you; I cannot let you go unpunished." God loves us too much to allow us to continue to disobey Him without consequences. Does it hurt Him more than it hurts us? I believe beyond a shadow of doubt that it does. Think about it, if God loved us so much (and He did) that He would send his only son (and He did) to die for us on a cross (and He did), then I am sure that it hurts Him deeply to see his children (us) have to go through his discipline. He doesn't like it! Let's save both God and ourselves the pain of having to endure something that neither enjoys, "to be disciplined by our Father." How can we do that? Great question. Do not disobey the Father!

From the sands of Iraq,

God bless!

Restoration

Scripture: *"But in that coming day, all who destroy you will be destroyed, and all your enemies will be sent into exile. Those who plunder you will be plundered, and those who attack you will be attacked. I will give you back your health and heal your wounds, says the Lord."*

(Jeremiah 30: 16 NLT)

DEVOTIONAL

Now here is a message that I'm sure that Jeremiah didn't mind preaching, telling the people that their disciplined time was over and that God was going to restore them to a place of prominence. I can relate! I, too, feel good when God speaks to me to tell (even you right now) that your time of suffering, your time of struggle, your time of being down is over. OVER, yes, over! Listen to what God is saying to you through me and the prophet Jeremiah today: "all who destroy you will be destroyed, and all your enemies will be sent into exile. Those who plunder you will be plundered, and those who attack you will be attacked. I will give you back your health and heal your wounds." (Lord, have mercy!) Do you understand what I am saying? Some of you have been in your darkest hour but it's over. Some of you have been under severe attack from your enemies, but that's over, too. God is sending your enemies into exile to bother you no more. Some of you have been struggling with an illness, but God has said, "I will give you back your health and heal your wounds. Today is your day of deliverance. Now do this, shout out loud these words: "PRAISE THE LORD!" Did you do it? Okay, maybe you should go outside and shout out these words, rather than making noise in your office. However, if you're feeling it, do it!

From the sands of Iraq,

God bless!

Chaplain King also served with the United States Marines.

Rebuilding

Scripture: *"In the past I uprooted and tore down this nation. I overthrew it, destroyed it, and brought disaster upon it. But in the future I will plant it and build it up, says the Lord."*

(Jeremiah 31:28 NLT)

DEVOTIONAL

If you don't believe that all is in God's hand, read what God said to the people through his prophet. "I uprooted;" "I tore down;" "I overthrew it;" "I destroyed it;" "I brought disaster upon it." Get the picture? God is in control! Nothing happens without his knowledge; nothing catches Him by surprise; nothing is out of his control. He made it clear to his people that their lives were in his hand and the manner in which they responded to his instructions made all the difference in how things happened in their lives. Do you think it is different with us today? It's not! God is in control of it all, including the economy, our jobs, our relationships, our money, our lives, especially if we are Christians. How we respond to his instructions can make all the difference in the world regarding how things happen in our lives. Yes, God said through Jeremiah, "In the past I uprooted and tore down ... I overthrew it, destroyed it, and brought disaster upon it." However, don't stop reading, for the last part of what He said is the best part of all. He is saying it to you: "But in the future I will plant it and build it up." That's right! You may feel that you have been uprooted, torn down, overthrown, destroyed, and brought to disaster, but listen one more time: "in the future I will plant it and build it up." Who is He talking about? Good question ...YOU!

From the sands of Iraq,

God bless!

"If a baby dies,
will the baby go to heaven?"

Godless Ideas

Scripture: *"Do not waste time arguing over godless ideas and old wives' tales. Spend your time and energy in training yourself for spiritual fitness."*

(I Timothy 4:7 NLT)

DEVOTIONAL

Time is precious and valuable, and we should not waste it. How many times have you been asked questions that really have nothing to do with salvation? If we are not careful, we can get distracted by what Paul called "godless ideas and old wives' tales." Remember that the devil's sole job and purpose is to get you off track from what God wants you to do. He will use every trick in the book to get you frustrated, discouraged, and doubting God and his word. Don't fall for it! There are those out there who will do anything to see if they can get you to doubt what you have believed all your life. Why? They want to confuse you and to steal your joy. People have asked me questions such as, "Once you are saved are you always saved?" I usually answer this way, "Just make sure that you *are* saved and you are okay." Or, I've been asked, "If a baby dies, will the baby go to heaven?" Usually I will answer, "God will take care of the baby. You just make sure that if you die, *you* will go to heaven." This is exactly what Paul meant when he said, "Do not waste time arguing over godless ideas and old wives' tales." In other words, don't get caught up in God's business, but make sure that you are in "spiritual training" all the time so that when you are faced with difficult choices, tough situations, difficult people, and challenging circumstances, you are "spiritually equipped" and ready for battle.

From the sands of Iraq,

God bless!

"God knows exactly what you need."

God's Strength

Scripture: *"You are the one who rules the oceans. When their waves rise in fearful storms, you subdue them."*

(Psalm 89:9-13 NLT)

DEVOTIONAL

I tell you, my friends, God knows exactly what we need, when we need it, and what we need to hear. And He knows the right scripture to point us to in order to put our mind at ease. I have been listening to some of the news lately, and if I were not a praying man, I would be worried stiff. What about you? Are you finding yourself worrying about what you are hearing DAILY on TV from our trusted news media? Have you been hearing all the negative talk about the great depression and the bottom falling out of our economy? I know you have. Well, let me help you stop worrying and being concerned about what you are hearing from people who are not in control of anything. Listen to what the psalmist said and then tell me whether or not we have anything to worry about: "You are the one who rules the oceans. When their waves rise in fearful storms, you subdue them. You are the one who crushed the great sea monster. You scattered your enemies with your mighty arm. The heavens are yours, and the earth is yours; everything in the world is yours--you created it all. You created north and south. Mount Tabor and Mount Hermon praise your name. Powerful is your arm! Strong is your hand! Your right hand is lifted high in glorious strength." Now, after reading how powerful, awesome, wonderful, and mighty our God is, tell me that we have anything to worry about. I thought so, you agree with me!

From the sands of Iraq,

God bless!

"God places us
at a particular job. . .
to let His light shine
through us."

Bosses

Scripture*: "Christians who are slaves should give their masters full respect so that the name of God and his teaching will not be shamed."*

(I Timothy 6:1 NLT)

DEVOTIONAL

If you have ever wondered how you should work for bosses who may or may not be Christians, I Timothy 6:1 will answer your question. The bottom line is this: "show full respect so that the name of God and his teaching will not be shamed." Difficult, yes, but it is necessary. You see my friends, as Christians we work for the Lord and not for man/woman. Our commitment is to God and not to our earthly bosses. When God places us at a particular job, it is to let his light shine through us to the point that we will be ministering to others. Paul discusses this when he writes, "Christians who are slaves should give their masters full respect so that the name of God and his teaching will not be shamed." He is not talking about "slavery," but he's talking about those who are over us as our employers. These are our supervisors, the individuals who sign our fitness reports or our evaluations.

He is saying that as Christians we should work in such a way that our life and our work habits are a sermon. Is this a challenge at times? You bet it is! There are times when we work for some very difficult bosses: bosses who abuse us, treat us like "slaves," and disrespect us as human beings. Yet Paul says to "give them full respect so that the name of God and his teaching will not be shamed." If you are working for one of those difficult bosses and you find yourself not wanting to show him/her respect, remember this: "God fights your battles" and He will deal with your ungodly, unholy, disrespectful, and mean boss. He knows what you are going through and He knows how to handle your situation. Stay encouraged!

From the sands of Iraq,

God bless!

Money

Scripture: *"For the love of money is at the root of all kinds of evil. And some people, craving money, have wandered from the faith and pierced themselves with many sorrows."*

(I Timothy 6:10 NLT)

DEVOTIONAL

Money, money, money! I remember hearing a radio preacher once say, "The Bible says the love of money is the root of all evil, but I say the lack of money is the root of all evil." We have to be careful in this day and time that we do not ascribe to this philosophy. When we become so focused on "money" that we lose sight of God, then money has become our god and that is "the root of all kinds of evil." Even in this day of budget shortages, cutbacks, layoffs, job losses, and all the other things that are facing us, we must keep the faith in the one who has always sustained us: God. Money, or the making of money, cannot become our focal point. Remember, God has warned us that He is a jealous God and that we should have "no other God before Him." So, let's be careful and mindful that we do not fall into the trap of becoming so "materialistic" that we become less "God-listic." (I know, this is not a word, but you get the point.) Let us not be guilty of what Paul said in I Timothy 6:10, "And some people, craving money, have wandered from the faith and pierced themselves with many sorrows."

From the sands of Iraq,

God bless!

"His faithful promises are your armor and protection."

Sunshine

Scripture: *"Those who live in the shelter of the Most High will find rest in the shadow of the Almighty."*

(Psalm 91:1 NLT)

DEVOTIONAL

Many scriptures bless my heart, uplift my spirit, and just make my day a bright and sunshiny day. It does not matter what my day is like or what kind of day I'm having, Psalm 91 does miracles for me every time I read it. Listen to it, heed its words, and let it speak to you now. Take a deep breath and stand by for your blessing! Here goes:

> Those who live in the shelter of the Most High will find rest in the shadow of the Almighty. This I declare of the Lord; He alone is my refuge, my place of safety; He is my God and I am trusting Him. For He will rescue you from every trap [WOW, my word] and protect you from the fatal plague [WOW AGAIN, my words]. He will shield you with his wings. He will shelter you with his feathers. His faithful promises are your armor and protection. Do not be afraid of the terrors of the night, nor fear the dangers of the day, nor dread the plague that stalks in darkness, nor the disaster that strikes at midday. Though a thousand fall at your side, though ten thousand are dying around you, these evils will not touch you. But you will see it with your eyes; you will see how the wicked are punished. If you make the Lord your refuge, if you make the Most High your shelter, no evil will conquer you; no plague will come near your dwelling. For He orders his angels to protect you wherever you go. They will hold you with their

207

hands to keep you from striking your foot on a stone. [It's long but don't stop reading; it gets better, my words!] You will trample down lions and poisonous snakes; you will crush fierce lions and serpents under your feet! The Lord says I will rescue those who love me. I will protect those who trust in my name. When they call on me, I will answer, [see what I mean, my words] I will be with them in trouble. I will rescue them and honor them. I will satisfy them with a long life and give them my salvation.

Now, tell me that you were not blessed and encouraged by reading this psalm.

From the sands of Iraq,

God bless!

Promise

Scripture: *"Please pray to the Lord your God for us. As you know, we are only a tiny remnant compared to what we were before. Beg the Lord your God to show us what to do and where to go.... May the Lord your God be a faithful witness against us if we refuse to obey whatever He tells us to do!"*

(Jeremiah 42:2-5 NLT)

DEVOTIONAL

Be careful when you make a promise to God, because He will remember what you promised. Very often when we find ourselves in trouble, we will say, "Lord, if you only help me out of this one I will never do it again." We make promises in the heat of trouble that we forget about as soon as our troubles are over. We must be very careful to keep our promises to God. As I stated, He will remember what we promised and if we break the promise there could and will be serious consequences.

The children of Israel went to the prophet Jeremiah and asked him to "Please pray to the Lord your God for us.... Beg the Lord your God to show us what to do and where to go." They wanted God to tell them whether to go to Egypt or to stay where they were. Furthermore, they made this promise or oath: "May the Lord your God be a faithful witness against us if we refuse to obey whatever He tells us to do!" They said, "whether we like it or not, we will obey the Lord our God to whom we send you with our plea." Jeremiah said he would do it, but he warned them not to go back on their word/promise/oath. If they did, God would punish them for doing so. They didn't listen and the punishment was severe.

Please keep this in mind the next time you make a promise an oath or give your word to God. Don't forget the promise that you make, because God won't forget.

From the sands of Iraq,

God bless!

"Where people end up
when it comes to eternity
is up to them and God."

Fools

Scripture: *"When arguing with fools, don't answer their foolish arguments, or you will become as foolish as they are."*

(Proverbs 26:4-5 NLT)

DEVOTIONAL

At first glance, the above scripture may sound like a contradiction, but it's not. The focus here is on the "fool," and not the one with whom the "fool" is arguing. We have to be sure that we do not put ourselves in the position of arguing about "foolish" things, yet at the same time we must ensure that such foolish things are addressed correctly. This is not for our sake, but for the sake of those who are confused. For example, just today I was asked the question, "If you Christians [did you get that, "you Christians"?] are correct, then are you saying that everyone else is going to hell?" This is exactly what the Lord is talking about. Don't get caught up or pulled into a conversation/argument about whether or not a person of another religion is going to hell. Where people end up when it comes to eternity, is up to them and God. However, if this type of question is asked and you find yourself in a discussion/argument such as this, verse five applies. Answer the question in a firm, steadfast, unmovable way, out of love, concerning what you believe as a Christian. Be steadfast and unmovable that Jesus is the way, the truth, and the light, and that NO ONE comes to the Father without going through Christ. If we do not answer these types of questions in a firm and committed way, we could allow the person to "become wise" in his or her own estimation.

From the sands of Iraq,

God bless!

From left, SgtMaj Green, Chaplain King and SgtMaj Smith.

Example

Scripture: *"Such people claim they know God, but they deny Him by the way they live."*

(Titus 1:16 NLT)

DEVOTIONAL

If you think that the way you live does not make a strong statement about how you feel about God, then I invite you to read Titus 1:16 again. How you and I live as Christians does make a difference, not only to people, but to God as well. How we live says to others and to God whether we "deny" Him (God) or "affirm" Him (God). Our daily living tells others that we believe in the God we serve, in the word that He left us to read, and in the course that He directs for our lives. Paul said plainly to Titus that those who "rebel against right teaching engage in useless talk and deceive people" and have turned families away from the truth. You and I must always live in such a way that we teach others the true way of God by the life we lead and the life that we live.

Remember, you are the ONLY Bible that some people will ever open up to read. Be sure that the word of God which lives in you is coming out in a way that is pleasing to God. If it is pleasing to God, it will be accepted by others. If it is pleasing to God and others don't accept it, that is okay and you are on safe grounds.

From the sands of Iraq,

God bless!

Chaplain King visits with a local Hindu leader in Mauritius.

Copycats

Scripture: *"But Zedekiah did what was evil in the Lord's sight, just as Jehoiakim had done."*

(Jeremiah 52:2 NLT)

DEVOTIONAL

"Well, everyone else is doing it, so why shouldn't I? We have always done it this way, so why change now? Why do I have to be different?" These are common comments that I have heard so many times. But here is something to think about! Because something has been done a certain way doesn't mean that you have to continue doing it that way. Because everyone else is doing it, doesn't mean that it is right. Also, it is okay to be different, especially when you are being different for Christ. After all, Christ was different and He didn't continue the status quo. So what if you are changing? If you're changing for Christ's sake, change. It is always better, and more advantageous, to do things God's way and please Him rather than to continue to do things the same old ungodly way and incur the wrath of God.

Zedekiah, the reigning king of Israel, had a chance to make a great name for himself and to make things better for his people. Instead, the name that he made for himself was this: "he did what was evil in the Lord's sight, just as Jehoiakim had done." He followed in the footsteps of Jehoiakim, the evil king who had ruled before him. The result was that God "banished them from his presence and sent them into exile."

Now, I don't know about you, but I don't want to be banished by God and sent into exile. What about you? If you don't like the idea of exile, do the right thing as God dictates.

From the sands of Iraq,

God bless!

"It's not about our past,
our righteousness,
our goodness,
or our kindness."

Mercy

DEVOTIONAL

I am often asked, "Why are you so adamant about your belief in Christ, and what is the reason for your joy and praise?" I love it when I am asked those questions. It gives me a chance to explain a concept that just blows my mind. This concept says "when God our Savior revealed his kindness and love, He saved us [me], not because of the righteous things we [I] had done, but because of his mercy." You see, my friends, that's what it is all about. It's not about our past, our righteousness, our goodness, or our kindness. In fact, let the truth be told, we are not righteous at all. It is all about God showing us his kindness, love, and mercy. He loved us so much that He sacrificed or sent his one and only Son to give his life for you and me. God knows that even at our best, we are at our worst. Yet, God decided to reveal to us just how kind and loving He was by saving us and showing us his mercy. Now, when you think about that truthful concept, how can you not be adamant about your relationship with Christ? When you think about God saving us, despite ourselves, it gives you a reason to feel joy and to give Him praise. I don't know about you, but that is reason enough for me to praise Him until the cows come home. Want to join me? Go ahead, praise Him now for what He has done for you.

From the sands of Iraq,

God bless!

"Fire goes out
for the lack of fuel,
and quarrels disappear
when gossip stops."

Gossip

Scripture: *"Fire goes out for lack of fuel, and quarrels disappear when gossip stops."*

(Proverbs 26:20 NLT)

DEVOTIONAL

Have you ever heard the old saying, "if you don't throw fuel on a fire, it won't burn?" Or maybe you heard it this way, "don't throw fuel on a lighted fire?" Regardless, both statements are in line with the words of the writer of Proverbs 26:20. If we don't gossip, it is true that quarrels, arguments, fights, and heated disputes will lose their flame. Think of how many lives have been destroyed because either we were gossiping, or we joined in with the gossip, or we didn't stand up against gossiping, or we laughed at the gossiping, or we participated in the gossip in some way, shape, form, or fashion. Many hurt feelings could have been avoided if we had only remembered that God does not like gossip and those who participate in it are not pleasing God.

The next time you are in your space, out with friends, standing around talking to co-workers, and someone starts up a "gossiping" conversation, I challenge you to do one of the following. (Only one, well, if you feel led, you can do more than one.) (1) Speak out against gossiping. (2) Challenge those who are doing the gossiping to share the gossip with the person or persons that they are gossiping about. (3) Walk away from the gossiping conversation. (4) Go to the defense of the one being gossiped about. (5) Remind the gossipers that "he/she who is without sin, be the first to cast the stone." (Now be careful with this one because we have some "perfect" folks out there who will pick up a stone and throw it ... at least they are perfect in their own mind). If you select one, two, three, or more of these, I can almost guarantee you that those doing the gossiping will look at you funny and then start gossiping about you. But guess what? You will have been an excellent example of Proverbs 26:20: "Fire goes out for lack of fuel, and quarrels disappear when gossip stops." You would have stopped the gossip by not participating. Don't worry; God will deal with those who gossip about you!

From the sands of Iraq,

God bless!

False Prophets

Scripture: *"Your Prophets have said so many foolish things, false to the core. They did not try to hold you back from exile by pointing out your sins. Instead, they painted false pictures, filling you with false hope."*

(Lamentations 2:14 NLT)

DEVOTIONAL

Jeremiah is known as the weeping prophet because he was grieved and cried over the condition of his people. It broke his heart to see the suffering of his people, especially when he knew that their suffering could have been avoided had they simply listened to the right people instead of the wrong people. We have to be careful that we do not fall prey to false prophets, teachers, preachers, evangelists, schoolteachers, and so forth, and end up on the wrong side of eternity. Remember the words and warning of Jesus: "not everyone that says Lord, Lord will enter into the kingdom of heaven." Also, remember that the Bible warns us that in the latter days there will be "false Prophets" who will not tell us the truth or tell us about our sins, but who instead will "paint false pictures, filling us with false hope." How can we avoid this terrible mistake? Good question.

1. Read the Bible for yourself.
2. Test what you hear by the word of God.
3. Don't trust those who tell you that your sins are okay because times and things have changed and everybody is doing it these days.

Remember the words of the songwriter: "my hope is built on nothing less than Jesus' blood and righteousness, I dare not trust the sweetest frame but wholly lean on Jesus name. On Christ the solid Rock, I stand, all other ground is sinking sand." If we stand on the word of God, we are standing on solid ground, and we will not be deceived by false prophets.

From the sands of Iraq,

God bless!

Separation

Scripture: *"For the Lord does not abandon anyone forever. Though He brings grief, He also shows compassion according to the greatness of His unfailing love. For He does not enjoy hurting people or causing them sorrow."*

(Lamentations 3:31-33 NLT)

DEVOTIONAL

This is a scripture of hope. When you feel abandoned by God or you are being disciplined by Him, remember that his discipline will not last forever. Discipline is not an enjoyable thing and while we are going through it, the pain can seem unbearable. But, remember that "though He [God] brings grief, He also shows compassion according to the greatness of his unfailing love." Paul asked, "Can anything separate us from Christ's love?" He said, "neither death nor life, neither angels nor demons, neither our fears for today nor our worries about tomorrow, not even the powers of hell can separate us from God's love. No power in the sky above or in the earth below, indeed, nothing in all of creation will ever be able to separate us from the love of God that is revealed in Christ Jesus our Lord." That is what Jeremiah meant when he said, "For the Lord does not abandon anyone forever. Though He brings grief, He also shows compassion according to the greatness of his unfailing love. For He does not enjoy hurting people or causing them sorrow." It grieves God to discipline us as his children, but He must discipline us because He loves us too much to allow us to keep going down the wrong path of unrighteousness or to stay on the path of sin.

From the sands of Iraq,

God bless!

"The Lord sees all these things."

Witness

Scripture: *"If people crush underfoot all the prisoners of the land, if they deprive others of their rights in defiance of the Most High, if they twist justice in the courts, doesn't the Lord see all these things?"*

(Lamentations 3:34-37 NLT)

DEVOTIONAL

Today's scripture is a clear indication that we had better pay close attention to how we treat one another. Why? "The Lord sees all these things." Injustice, mistreatment of others, ridiculing one another, twisting justice in the courts, depriving others of their rights will not go un-noticed nor will our actions go unpunished. God is watching everything we do and every action we take. Whatever we do in this life will not only come up again in the next life, but there will be a day of reckoning now. In other words, we will reap what we sow! We cannot deprive others of their human and God-given rights without being in "defiance of the Most High." Are you sure you want to put yourself in that position? I don't know about you, but I most certainly do not. To do so is to place oneself directly in opposition to God, and trust me, you don't want to do that. I'd much rather be on God's side than against Him. Bottom line, do the right thing toward one another and toward God's people.

From the sands of Iraq,

God bless!

"Jesus knew, exactly what
was happening."

The Lord's Permission

Scripture: *"Who can command things to happen without the Lord's permission? Does not the Most High send both calamity and good? Then why should we, mere humans, complain when we are punished for our sins?"*

(Lamentations 3:37-39 NLT)

DEVOTIONAL

It may seem strange to use Lamentation 3:37-39 on the eve of Easter and for Good Friday, but I think it is very befitting. You see on Good Friday, Christ put Himself in the place of a sinner (us) and endured the shame, humiliation, and pain of the cross. Nothing that happened on Good Friday happened by accident, but God knew, and his Son Jesus knew, exactly what was happening, and both knew it before it ever happened. Furthermore, it happened, not only with their knowledge, but it also happened with their "permission." That is why these three verses are so relevant at this time. Truly, think about it, "Who can command things to happen without the Lord's permission?" The answer is simple: "no one." No one can command things to happen without the Lord's permission and no one can command things to happen to you and me without the "Lord's permission."

When Jesus died on the cross on Good Friday, He turned what Satan thought was bad into what was "good." Good Friday was painful to Christ in more than one way; it was painful physically and spiritually. It was painful physically because of the nails in his hands, spear in his side, and thorns on his brow. In addition, He contended with the hot heat beating down on his body. It was painful spiritually because He had put Himself in the place of a sinner, and for the first time His Father had to look away because God cannot look upon sin without dealing with it. That is why the Bible says, "For God made Christ, who never sinned, to be the offering for our sin, so that we could be made right with God through Christ."

Yes, Lamentations 3:37-39 is very fitting at this time! Listen to it again, "Who can command things to happen without the Lord's permission? Does not the Most High send both calamity and good? Then why should we, mere humans, complain when we are punished for our sins." You get it? If Christ was punished for "our" sin and He Himself had never sinned, then why shouldn't we be "punished for our sins?" We have nothing to complain about. Think about it!

From the sands of Iraq,

God bless!

Resurrected Attitude

Scripture: *"That is why I am boldly asking a favor of you. I could demand it in the name of Christ because it is the right thing for you to do. But because of our love, I prefer simply to ask you. Consider this as a request from me –Paul, an old man and now also a prisoner for the sake of Christ Jesus."*

(Philemon 1: 8-9 NLT)

DEVOTIONAL

Having a "resurrected" attitude is a great way to celebrate Christ's resurrection. By this I mean to wipe the slate clean by forgiving that one person or persons who have wronged you in the past, but whom you haven't quite found the strength to forgive. Christ has given us the power to forgive, and He did it on Easter Sunday. In today's scripture reading, Paul calls in a favor for "my child Onesimus" who had not been "much use" in the past. Paul does not explain exactly what he means when he says that Onesimus has not been "much use" in the past, but whatever the case, Paul was calling in a favor from those he had favor with, mainly Philemon. It is believed by some that Onesimus was a runaway slave, and that Paul is writing the owner (Philemon) asking that he "show kindness" when Onesimus returns. Paul describes Onesimus as "no longer like a slave," but a "beloved brother." Regardless of the reason, or what Onesimus had or had not done, Paul is calling in a favor of kindness and forgiveness. Christ's resurrection calls us to show kindness and forgiveness toward those who have wronged us. Remember the words of Jesus on the cross, "Father forgive them for they know not what they do." We, too, as difficult as it may be, must pray those words "Father, forgive them for they know not what they do." Those words are God's way of "asking us for a favor" on behalf of his children, even those who are not of the fold.

From the sands of Iraq,

God bless!

"Aren't you glad that you have an 'angel in your outfield?'"

Angels

DEVOTIONAL

I saw a movie once entitled *Angels in the Outfield*. It was about a baseball team that couldn't win a baseball game if it was given to them. Then all of a sudden the team started winning every game they played. When the sports writers and others inquired as to what had changed, they discovered that each team member had an "angel in the outfield" who assisted the player by running, catching, and anything else the team needed to win each game. Just think about it! The writer of Hebrews 1:14 talks about our "angel in the outfield" (so to speak) and how our angels are "only servants--spirits sent to care for people who will inherit salvation." Aren't you glad that you have an "angel in your outfield" and that your angel is sent by God to care for you? But then this is only if you are one of those people/individuals "who will inherit salvation." Bottom line, be sure that you are on the winning team of Christ. If you are, then be certain that your "angel" is in the outfield of your life and that your "angel" has been sent by Christ to care for you because you are one who "will inherit salvation." Each time you go outside, go to work, drive your automobile, ride on a plane or train, or just walk or run for exercise, you have an angel (or angels) watching over you. Hallelujah! Praise the Lord! Shout about it. Your angel is watching over you at the guidance and direction of Christ! Again, be sure that you are on the right team: Christ's!

From the sands of Iraq,

God bless!

"…I'm pretty convinced that no one dared mess with her too much once they found out that 'her brother was a Navy Captain.'"

Brotherly Love

Scripture: *"So now Jesus and the ones He makes holy have the same Father. That is why Jesus is not ashamed to call them His brothers and sister. For He said to God, I will proclaim Your name to My brothers and sisters. I will praise You among Your assembled people."*

(Hebrews 2:11-12 NLT)

DEVOTIONAL

Several years ago I met a young lady that I adopted as "my little sister." She's now a Commander in the United States Navy, and I have mentored and watched her career grow over the years. Most people, even those who know both of us well, are unaware that she's really not my "blood" sister. We refer to each other simply as "my little sister" or "my big brother."

Before deployment in 2006, we had the pleasure of going through two weeks of combat training. As usual, we introduced each other as "my little sister" and "my big brother." One day, I overheard some of the other military personnel saying, "Did you know that her brother is a Navy Captain?" Now, I can't say for certain that she got special treatment, but I'm pretty convinced that no one dared mess with her too much once they found out that "her brother was a Navy Captain." Am I special? No! Does rank have its privileged? Yes! Does it help to know someone with a high ranking? Yes! To the other military personnel Janet, my little sister, had a high ranking officer as a brother and, as such, they were a little bit careful how they treated her.

It is very similar but on a MUCH larger scale when it comes to Jesus.

Because we are his, because we are "the ones He makes holy" and "have the same Father," we are now his brothers and sisters. As such, we get special privileges that others may not get. As Jesus' brothers and sisters, we have an inside connection that makes us special, respected and protected. That is why Jesus, our elder brother, said to his Father (God), now our Father, "I will proclaim your name (God) to My brothers and sisters. I will praise you among your assembled people." Now, I don't know about you, but I think it's pretty cool to have a "big brother" that is the creator of all things, in charge of all things and controls all things. Who can have a greater brother than "Jesus?" I may be a pretty cool "big brother" to Janet, but Jesus is a much cooler brother. Guess what's next? Once you accept Him into your heart, He becomes your "elder brother" and THAT'S PRETTY COOL!

From the sands of Iraq,

God bless!

Refuge

Scripture: *"For this good news that God has prepared this rest has been announced to us just as it was to them. But it did them no good because they didn't share the faith of those who listened to God. For only we who believe can enter His rest. As for the others, God said, 'In My anger I took an oath: They will never enter My place of rest.'"*

(Hebrews 4:2-3 NLT)

DEVOTIONAL

What good is it to have a beautiful house waiting for you and you miss out on living in it because you refuse to believe that it is yours? How would you feel if you found out two days too late that someone had donated $3 million to you, but you didn't get it because you refused to believe the messenger two days earlier? I think we both know the answer to both questions, you'd feel pretty bad. At least I know that I would!

Well, think about this good news! God has prepared rest for all of us and the only thing required of us is to "share the faith of those who listened to God." In other words, BELIEVE! The question may be asked "what rest is the writer of Hebrews talking about?" Good question and here is the answer. He's talking about rest in this life and rest in the life to come. Jesus said, "Come to me, all of you who are weary and carry heavy burdens, and I will give you rest."

We can have rest from our daily worries, rest from our daily fears, rest from mental torture and torment, rest from nagging folks, rest from anything that we want. The key is to "share the faith of those who listened to God." You see, my friends, there are those who listen to God's word based upon faith and there are those who do not listen to God period. Those who listen to God's word will find rest in this life and the life to come. Those who do not listen to God's word will not find rest in this life or in the life to come. So which do you want? Rest in both worlds or no rest in both worlds? You have to choose one or the other. I know my choice! What about you?

From the sands of Iraq,

God bless!

Understanding

Scripture: *"For we do not have a high priest who is unable to sympathize with our weaknesses, but One who has been tested in every way as we are, yet was without sin. Therefore let us approach the throne of grace with boldness, so that we may receive mercy and find grace to help us at the proper time."*

(Hebrews 4:15-16 NLT)

DEVOTIONAL

You think Jesus doesn't understand your struggles? Think again because He does! Do you think Jesus hasn't dealt with the same temptations that you are and have been dealing with? Think again because He has! The writer of Hebrews plainly states that "we do not have a high priest who is UNABLE (all caps my doing) to sympathize with our weaknesses, but One who has been tested in EVERY WAY (all caps my doing) as we are, yet without sin." Yes, Jesus understands and knows EXACTLY what you are dealing with, the temptations that you are facing and the trials and tribulations that come your way. He understands, he's dealt with them and He knows how to assist you in overcoming everything that you are facing. How? He has been there. Who is better equipped to assist you than one who has walked in your shoes, faced the same temptations and "yet without sin?" The answer is "our high priest" named Jesus!

He can handle your problems, so why not trust Him to do so. We trust people who have no power, put our faith in things that can't help us, and systems that fail us. Why not change our tactics and trust one that has passed EVERY test, every trial, every tribulation, every temptation and every tough situation? Jesus can be trusted and He has proven that

He can be. So why not do what verse 16 says, "therefore let us approach the throne of grace with BOLDNESS [all caps my doing], so that we may receive MERCY [all caps my doing] and find GRACE [all caps my doing] to help us at the proper time."

Try it right now! I dare you! I'm confident that you will not be disappointed, you will not be let down, you will not be betrayed, you will not be overcome, YOU WILL BE VICTORIOUS! As we used to say down home when I was growing up, "I double-dog dare you to try Him!" My friends, your high priest [Jesus] is the best and most trust worthy person that you will ever meet. Try Him today!

From the sands of Iraq,

God bless!

Covenant

Scripture: *"But this is the covenant that I will make with the house of Israel after those days, says the Lord: I will put My laws into their minds, and I will write them on their hearts, and I will be their God, and they will be My people. And each person will not teach his fellow citizen, and each his brother, saying Know the Lord, because they will all know me, from the least to the greatest of them. For I will be merciful to their wrongdoing, and I will never again remember their sins."*

(Hebrews 8:10-12 NIV)

DEVOTIONAL

Have you ever made a covenant, contract, or promise to someone and broken it? It didn't feel too good, did it? Have you ever been disappointed by someone who made a promise and didn't keep his or her word? When this happened, I bet you were a little upset, weren't you? Have you ever listened to the words of someone else only to find out that these words were not exactly the truth? In fact, the words were totally false and you were disappointed because you had trusted that person?

Well, this will never happen when you put your trust in Jesus. He makes a lasting covenant that can never be broken. God is true to His word, and He keeps His word every time. You don't have to depend upon anyone to tell you what the Lord is saying to you or what He has for you to do. Why? Because He will tell you Himself. Listen to what He said, "I will put My laws into their minds, and I will write them on their hearts." When we accept Christ as our personal savior, He puts his laws in our mind and writes them on our hearts. We can't go wrong as long as we listen to "his laws in our mind" and follow the laws of God that have been "written on our hearts."

Now, I want you to stop and pay special attention to the last thing that I'm about to say because this could mean eternal freedom for you. This is what the writer of Hebrews says Christ will do for everyone who believes in Jesus: "For I will be merciful to their wrongdoing, and I will NEVER [all caps my doing] again REMEMBER their sins." You see, my brothers and sisters, we have too much to lose by not trusting in Christ and we have EVERYTHING to gain by doing so. We serve a "merciful" God who remembers our sins no more and wipes the slate clean. If God wipes the slate clean, why do you dwell on your past mistakes or past failures? There is no need to do so ... remember what He (God) said, "I will be merciful to their [yours and mine] wrongdoing, and I will NEVER again remember their sins."

From the sands of Iraq,

God bless!

Guarantees

Scripture: *"And just as it is appointed for people to die once—and after this, judgment—so also the Messiah, having been offered once to bear the sins of many, will appear a second time, not to bear sin, but to bring salvation to those who are waiting for Him."*

(Hebrews 9:27-28 HCSB)

DEVOTIONAL

There are not many things that are guaranteed in life, but Hebrews 9:27-28 guarantees a couple of things that we can be certain about. One, we all have an appointment with death, and two, we all must stand before God to be judged. I don't know about you, but these two things influence my life daily when it comes to how I live and how I treat others. Death does not scare me because I know whose I am and I am certain about my belief in Christ. Therefore, I'm sealed and I am one of those who is "waiting for Him" to return. The number two certainty (I must admit) scares me at times: the judgment of God! I am certain that there have been times when I failed the judgment test and have had to repent for my actions.

However, another part of today's thought frees me from the fear of God's judgment and that is the knowledge that "the Messiah [Christ], having been offered once to bear the sins of many, will appear a second time, not to bear sin, but to bring salvation to those who are waiting for Him." Because of Christ's death I am free, forgiven, and washed clean. I look forward to that day when Christ will appear the "second time" and take me back with Him to that place where there is no more death, no more sorrow, no more tears, no more hardship, no more trials or tribulation. With this kind of assurance, how can you not stop right now and shout? Excuse me for a moment ... I'm back now! I had to take a moment and SHOUT! Would you like to shout with me? Let's do it together now. SHOUT "AMEN!"

From the sands of Iraq,

God bless!

Blind Faith

Scripture: *"Faith is the confidence that what we hope for will actually happen; it gives us assurance about things we cannot see. And it is impossible to please God without faith. Anyone who wants to come to Him must believe that God exists and that He rewards those who sincerely seek Him."*

(Hebrews 11:1-6 NLT)

DEVOTIONAL

I love it when someone says, "no one can have blind faith," or "how can you believe in something that you can't see?" First of all, I don't have blind faith! God has proven to me (and I hope to you also) over and over again that He is exactly who He says He is, and He can do exactly what He says He can do. Secondly, I usually will explain that everyone has "faith." It's just a matter of whether your faith is "blind" or "seeing." To have "blind faith" is to believe in the whatever. To have "seeing faith" is to believe in the God who created us, sustains us, and takes care of us.

Here's what I'm talking about. How many times have you gotten on a plane without checking the license of the pilot? Let me guess, every time! Okay, let me ask another question. How many times have you taken pills from doctors, nurses, or medical staff without asking to see their medical credentials? Let me guess again, every time! Okay, last question! How many times have you gone to a restaurant and ordered food without knowing where the food was grown, where it came from, or even if the person(s) who cooked the food put something in it that shouldn't be? By the way, this is a good reason to "bless your food every time before you eat." But let me guess anyway. Every time!

You see, my friends, this is what Hebrews 11:1 is talking about when the writer says, "Faith is the confidence that what we hope for will actually happen; it give us assurance about things we cannot see." We board a plane because we have "faith" that it's going to land safely! We take medication from medical personnel without seeing their credentials because we have "faith" that they are legit and that the medicine is going to work. We eat food from restaurants (without blessing it) because we have "faith" that the food has been properly tested, cooked, and treated, and that it will do us no harm. God has proven Himself time after time and has never been wrong.

The one with "blind faith" cannot explain who he/she believes in and cannot explain why things happen the way they do. My faith says I will board a plane, eat a meal (after blessing it), and take medicine without knowing anything about the doctor because "faith gives me assurance about things I cannot see." Why? Without it (faith), I cannot please God and I don't want to board a plane, eat a meal, or take any medication without pleasing God. What about you?

From the sands of Iraq,

God bless!

Faithfulness

Scripture: *"By faith Noah, after being warned about what was not yet seen, in reverence built an ark to deliver his family. By this he condemned the world and became an heir of the righteousness that comes by faith."*

(Hebrew 11:7 NAS)

DEVOTIONAL

"Build a *what* ... an *ark*? You mean you want me to build a boat on dry land? Are you kidding, Lord?" I don't know if Noah asked God this question or not when directed by God to build an ark on dry land. But, I can speak for myself (and probably you, too) when I say that there have been times when I have said "Are you kidding, Lord?" Laughter, strange stares, sarcastic jabs, whispering behind his back (and probably to his face also) are just a few things that I'm sure Noah had to endure while he followed God's orders.

You may not realize it, but you are and have been the key, as well as the glue, that has held things together for your family, co-workers, friends, nasty bosses, marriages, children, and so forth, all because you built an ark on dry land when there was no rain in the forecast, clouds in the sky, or mist in the air. Because you obeyed God, your marriage, family, and all those listed earlier received a blessing and their situation was changed or their lives were saved. When God directs you to do something (build an ark on dry land), do it regardless of who approves, follows, or disagrees with you.

Some may ask, "What would have happened if Noah had not obeyed

God?" He did, so the "what would have happened?" question is irrelevant. The point is this, do what God tells you to do, have faith in Him and his word, obey his every command, and you and many others will receive the blessings that He has for you. Do it in faith and trust the creator of the universe. You will not be disappointed.

From the sands of Iraq,

God bless!

The Race

Scripture: *"Therefore since we also have such a large cloud of witnesses surrounding us, let us lay aside every weight and the sin that so easily ensnares us, and run with endurance the race that lies before us, keeping our eyes on Jesus, the source and perfecter of our faith, who for the joy that lay before Him endured a cross and despised the shame, and has sat down at the right hand of God's throne."*

(Hebrew 12:1-2 HCSB)

DEVOTIONAL

Today's scripture reading points out several encouraging things. (1) We have a large crowd of cheerleaders and fans cheering for us as we run this Christian race. (2) If we "lay aside" (which means to rid ourselves of something) everything that holds us back, the backpack of burdens (and many other things) that we carry will be lighter and we can run the race easier and "with endurance." (3) Jesus is the "source" and "perfecter" of our faith, which means that as long as we depend upon Jesus as the "source" of our strength, we will never be without the strength and the things that we need to run a successful race. Also, since Jesus is the "perfecter" of our faith and the source of our strength, as long as we keep our eyes "fixed" on Him, He will give us the faith we need to endure this race from start to finish.

The next time you are feeling that the race is getting tough, look up into the cheering stands. Hear the loud cheers of support from those who have gone before you and have endured, and remember that you are not alone. Also, look up into the cheering stands and in the middle of the crowd you will see "Jesus" cheering the loudest. He will be shouting out commands, telling you to breathe in and breathe out ... to steady the pace ... to pace yourself ... to pass the baton to the next runner because you have done your part. Look up and see "Jesus" in the middle of the crowd saying that I ran this race before you so that I could tell you exactly how to run this race and win. Look up and see "Jesus" in the middle of the crowd (Can you see Him?) shouting out loud, "I was willing to die a shameful death on the cross because of the joy that I knew would be mine afterwards. I ran and now you can run with confidence, certainty, hope, joy, praise, and thanksgiving. You can run this race and YOU CAN WIN because 'I am the source of your strength.'"

Did you see Him in the crowd? Did you hear Him shouting out instructions to you telling you how to win the race? If you didn't, stop right now and listen. He's talking to you now!

From the sands of Iraq,

God bless!

Correction

Scripture: *"My son, do not take the Lord's discipline lightly, or faint when you are reproved by Him; for the Lord disciplines whom He loves, and punishes every son whom He receives. Endure it as discipline: God is dealing with you as sons."*

(Hebrews 12:5-7 HCSB)

DEVOTIONAL

I always had a hard time correcting my son. One concern was whether or not he would understand that I was doing it for his good and to make him a better person. I never said to him, "Now, this hurts me more than it hurts you," but there were times when I am certain that it did. Discipline is a necessary thing! It may not "be pleasant" as we receive or go through it, but when done by a loving father or parent, it truly is for "our good." I realize that there are some who have been abused by parents, and this is sad and wrong. God will never abuse you or me, but He will "discipline" us. This is precisely why the writer of Hebrews 12:5-7 says, "My son, do not take the Lord's discipline lightly, or faint when you are reproved by Him; for the Lord disciplines whom He loves, and punishes every son [daughter, too—my addition] whom He receives."

I didn't like it when my parents disciplined or punished me, and I am sure that my son didn't like it when I disciplined or punished him. But, I think he will not hesitate to admit that I love him and that good fatherly discipline has made him a better person. This is the point that the writer of Hebrews is trying to make to us: God loves us so much that He must discipline or punish us when we do wrong, fail to listen, do not adhere to his teachings, or neglect to follow his instructions.

He, too, doesn't like it but it must be done. Why? It's because "the Lord disciplines whom He loves." I am thankful for parents who corrected, disciplined, and at times punished me. I am also grateful to a God who loves me a trillion times more. As such, I will "endure it as discipline" and see it for what it is, "God dealing with me as his son." When it comes to being disciplined by God, I agree with David who said, "I would rather be in the hand of an angry God because even in his anger He is merciful."

From the sands of Iraq,

God bless!

Perfect Praise

Scripture: *"Therefore, through Him let us continually offer up to God a sacrifice of praise, that is, the fruit of our lips that confess His name."*

(Hebrews 13:15 HCSB)

DEVOTIONAL

I come from a faith tradition where "praise" is not only encouraged but expected. In my home church in Senatobia, Mississippi, we lift our hands, shout (out loud) amen, dance in the aisles, and respond to the word of God when it is being preached, taught, or read. Over the course of my military career, I have met individuals who have made sly remarks or poked fun at my worship style. That is "perfectly" okay because I have come to believe that "praise" is a "necessary" part of the worship experience. The writer, in his letter to the Hebrews, says, "Therefore, through Him let us continually offer up to God a sacrifice of praise, that is, the fruit of our lips that confess His name." I don' think others should (necessarily) praise God the way I do, but I do think that "praise" is necessary. Paul and Silas sang songs of praise to God during their imprisonment. Jesus said, when the Pharisees were trying to stop the crowd from "praising God joyfully with a loud voice" by keeping them quiet, "I tell you, if they were to keep silent, the stones would cry out." When the news of Jesus' birth was announced, "suddenly there was a multitude of the heavenly host with the angel, praising God." Believe me when I tell you that there is power in "praise." If people ask me why I praise God the way I do, I would answer them this way. Every time I "praise" Him, I forget about all of my problems, troubles, trials, and tribulations, and I focus totally on the many blessings that he (God) has done for me. You see, my listening friends, when I look back over my life and see where God has brought me, I have to open my mouth and "shout out praises" to Him. Watch out. I'm about to do it now. What? Shout out some "praises to God"! Would you like to join me? Come on, try it. Shout "Praise the Lord!" Oops, I know, I'm trying to get you to praise God the way I do. Sorry, but it does work! God bless and don't forget what the writer of Hebrews 13:15 said, "let us continually offer up to God a sacrifice of Praise."

From the sands of Iraq,

God bless!

Indecision

Scripture: *"Now, if any of you lacks wisdom, he should ask God, who gives to all generously and without criticizing, and it will be given to him. But let him ask in faith without doubting. For the doubter is like the surging sea, driven and tossed by the wind. That person should not expect to receive anything from the Lord. An indecisive man is unstable in all his ways."*

(James 1:5-8 HCSB).

DEVOTIONAL

"Why don't you make up your mind? One day you say this and the next day you say something totally different." Have you ever felt like or maybe even said these words to someone? Have you ever seen or worked for a person who couldn't make a decision and was as shaky as shifting sand? I have met people who change denominations and/or religious faith groups like water runs out of a faucet. We, Christians are not supposed to be like that and the key to not being such an "indecisive" person is to be sure that you do the first thing that James recommends, and that is to ask for wisdom.

This is the key to making the right decisions in life, making the right decision when it comes to choosing a church, a partner, a business ... or buying a house, car or anything else. James is clear, "If any of you lacks wisdom, he should ask God, who gives to all generously and without criticizing, and it will be given to him."

The problems with many of us are (1) we think we have the answers to many of our questions; (2) we think we know what to do in most situations; (3) we think we know how to handle most things in our life, and (4) we think we know exactly which direction to go. Therefore, we do things without first "asking God for wisdom." When we do this, we end up being "tossed by the wind" of uncertainty and running in all directions without a goal, aim, or clue as to what we are doing. James says "that person should not expect to receive anything from the Lord" because an "indecisive man [person—my word] is unstable in all his ways."

Here are several things to think about. (1) When you make decisions, do you ask God to "give you wisdom?" (2) Have you noticed that you have been indecisive at times and didn't or couldn't explain why? (3) Have you played musical church ... going from one church to another without finding a church home? (4) Have you found yourself running in all directions without a goal, aim, or clue as to what you were doing? Be honest with yourself, be honest with God, and then take James's advice and "ask God for wisdom." He will give it to you and the only thing He wants in return is for you to "ask in faith without doubting."

From the sands of Iraq,

God bless!

Talking Walls

Scripture: *"But be doers of the word and not hearers only, deceiving yourselves. Because if anyone is a hearer of the word and not a doer, he is like a man looking at his own face in a mirror; for he looks at himself, goes away, and right away forgets what kind of man he was. But the one who looks intently into the perfect law of freedom and perseveres in it, and is not a forgetful hearer but a doer who acts—this person will be blessed in what he does."*

(James 1:22-25 HCSB)

DEVOTIONAL

I once heard a minister preach a sermon entitled "If walls could talk." The minister asked his congregation, what would their walls say about them if they could talk and tell their story? I'd like to ask you a similar question: what kind of report card would you receive from your walls when it comes to you being a doer of the word, if your walls were able to speak? Would your walls confirm that you are a Christian in your home just as well as in the church? Would your walls verify your testimony when you say that you read your Bible and pray at home just like you do at church? Would your walls say that you are loving and kind to your family in private as well as in public? Would your walls say to you, "Come on, you know that you are faking it. Stop your playing with God?"

You see, my brothers and sisters, James 1:22-25 tells us to be "doers of the word and not hearers only." It is okay to read the Bible, go to church and listen to the preacher, and yes even read the "Thought for the Day" from Chaplain King, but if your actions are not consistent with your words, then you are a "hearer of the word and not a doer of the word." You may have heard me say this before, but God is interested in your "doing," not your "talking." Too many of us talk the word but do not live the word! I don't know about you, but I don't want to be described as a "hearer" only, because the description is not a pretty one. Listen to it: "if anyone is a hearer of the word and not a doer, he is like a man looking at his own face in a mirror; for he looks at himself, goes away, and right away forgets what kind of man he is." (Notice, I substituted the word "was" for "is" in that verse.) Does this sound like the kind of person you would like to be? Not me! Also remember this, there is a blessing in being a "doer of the word and not a hearer only," and this is the promised blessing, "This person will be blessed in what he does." Do you want to be blessed today? Then be a "doer of the word and not a hearer only."

God bless!

Pet Peeves

Scripture: *"If you really carry out the royal law prescribed in Scripture, 'You shall love your neighbor as yourself,' you are doing well. But if you show favoritism, you commit sin and are convicted by the law as transgressors. For whoever keeps the entire law, yet fails in one point, is guilty of breaking it all... Speak and act as those who will be judged by the law of freedom. For judgment is without mercy to the one who hasn't shown mercy. Mercy triumphs over judgment."*

(James 2:8-12 ESV)

DEVOTIONAL

Everyone has pet peeves. Sadly, even many churches and denominations (and Christians, too) have pet peeves when it comes to sin. Some will say "smoking is wrong;" others will say "cheating is wrong," while another will say "homosexuality is wrong" or "drinking is wrong." Everyone seems to have pet peeves, even in the church. I don't want to get into the discussion of whether or not the things I mentioned above are right and wrong, but I do want to point out what James said, "For whoever keeps the entire law, yet fails in ONE point [all caps my doing], is guilty of breaking it all." The next time you think about judging another person, ask yourself this question, "Have I kept the entire law?" If you are honest about it, you will answer that question this way: "No." No, I haven't kept the whole law, so instead of judging, I will "show mercy."

To show mercy does not mean that you or I cannot confront a person. To show mercy does not mean that you or I cannot encourage a brother or sister to stop sinning or stop the ungodly things that he/she may be doing. To show mercy does not mean that you or I cannot say to a brother or sister that "the Lord told me to tell you to stop transgressing his laws." But as James says, "Mercy triumphs over judgment" any day.

Aren't you glad that God shows mercy instead of judgment toward you on a daily basis? Well, maybe you are not, but I know that I am very grateful that God shows me "mercy" daily. My brothers and sisters, think about this, since none of us can truthfully say that we keep the "entire law" and therefore, we are guilty of being a "law breaker," wouldn't it be better to show mercy? Showing mercy toward others will guarantee you that God will show mercy toward you. Showing judgment toward others will guarantee you that God will show his judgment toward you. Which do you want to see from God, judgment or mercy? I know my choice; what about you?

God bless!

Works

Scripture: *"What good is it, my brothers, if someone says he has faith, but does not have works? Can his faith save him? If a brother or sister is without clothes and lacks daily food, and one of you says to them, 'Go in peace, keep warm, and eat well,' but you don't give them what the body needs, what good is it? In the same way faith, if it doesn't have works, is dead by itself."*

(James 2:14-18 HCSB)

DEVOTIONAL

I once read a story about a man having dinner with his family. He was praying at the dinner table, "Lord bless the homeless, bless those who are without food, give clothes to those who do not have clothes, provide for the sick." The man prayed on and on about the things that he wanted God to do for others. When he finally said "Amen," his son looked at his father and said "Dad, if I had your checkbook I would answer most of your prayer requests." Now, I don't know if this little child had ever heard of James 2:14-18, but I think he was right on target.

James says, "What good is it, my brothers, if someone says he has faith, but does not have works?" How often do we say to those in need, "Have faith, my brother; have faith, my sister," when we have the ability to show "faith" by assisting a brother or sister in need? We pray for the homeless, but how many times do we help the homeless? We pray for the sick, but how many times do we visit the sick? We pray for those who need clothes, but how many times do we do something about those without clothes by buying them some clothes? This is what

James means when he says, "If a brother or sister is without clothes and lacks daily food, and one of you says to them, 'Go in peace, keep warm and eat well,' but you don't give them what the body needs, what good is it? In the same way faith, if it doesn't have works, is dead by itself." Also, this is what he meant when he said, "Show me your faith without works, and I will show you faith from my works." James was talking about one who puts his/her faith into practice. He was also talking about one who gives lip service to faith but doesn't back it up with action. Which do you think impresses God, faith with lip service only or faith with works? Remember what James writes now, "faith, if it doesn't have works, is dead by itself." You guessed it, "faith with works," that is what impresses God!

God bless!

Joint Prayers

Scripture: *"Are any of you suffering hardships? You should pray. Are any of you happy? You should sing praises. Are any of you sick? You should call for the elders of the church to come and pray over you, anointing you with oil in the name of the Lord. Such a prayer offered in faith will heal the sick, and the Lord will make you well."*

(James 5:13-15 NLT).

DEVOTIONAL

Today's scripture reading addresses three areas affecting everyone: hardships, happiness, and sickness. Regardless of who you are, at one point or another you will experience one of these areas. James tells us what to do and how to handle each of them.

First, he says if you are "suffering hardship," pray. Pray your way through and out of your suffering. Don't give in to it but pray your way out of it. Sounds too simple? It is. Just do what James suggests: pray. Secondly, he says if you are "happy," sing praises. There is something about singing praises to God that releases the spirit. Even in the midst of a hard time, when we sing praises to God, it makes all the difference in the world. When you lift your voice and "sing praises to God," you tend to forget about your troubles, problems, and hardship. Don't worry about how you sound; just open your mouth and "make a joyful noise unto the Lord." Others may say that you sound terrible but God will hear your beautiful voice because of your humble heart. Thirdly, James says (and this one is my favorite): "if any of you are sick you should send for the elders of the church to come and pray over you, anointing you with oil in the name of the Lord." I love to visit my parishioners (and others, too) during times of suffering, happiness, and sickness. I don't love it because I love to see them suffering or sick, but I love to join with them in "prayer" together as we lift them up to God, anoint them with oil in the name of Jesus, and watch God make Satan mad. He makes Satan mad because when we are experiencing hardship, hard times, sickness or pain, the devil wants us to isolate ourselves, get off by ourselves and fall into a state of hopelessness, helplessness, and despair. But, when we "send for the elders of the church" or for other Christians to come join us, we have "double power" because "such prayers offered in faith will heal the sick, and the Lord will make us well."

Don't ever underestimate the power of "praying elders [or preachers]" and the anointing of oil. I can't speak for others but I know without a doubt that when I walk into a room of my parishioners and lay hands on them and anoint them with oil and pray in faith, God not only hears my prayer but He heals the person. Likewise, don't underestimate the power of your prayer when you pray in faith. If you need a partner in a particular area and you don't think that your prayer is getting through, let me know and I will join you. Together, we'll be victorious in the name of the Lord!

God bless!

Trust

Scripture: *"You love Him even though you have never seen Him. Though you do not see Him; and even now you are happy with a glorious, inexpressible joy. Your reward for trusting Him will be the salvation of your souls."*

(I Peter 1:8-9 NLT)

DEVOTIONAL

I have often told others that "I run no risk in trusting and loving God." If I am wrong (and I'm not), then when I die I am just a dead person and my life ended when I died. If I'm correct (and I am), then my reward is "the salvation of my soul" and I will spend eternity in the presence of God. Today's scripture reading encourages us to hold fast to what we believe, regardless of what others may or may not say or do. We live in a time when many are turning from the truth of believing in God and believing in his Son, Jesus. Many use the excuse, "how can you believe in a God that you have never seen?" Easy answer, because in doing so I receive the best reward that ANYONE can ever receive: "the salvation of my soul." Now, I don't know about you but that's a reward that I want. So, yes, I love God "even though I have never seen Him." What about you? Yes, "even now I am happy with a glorious inexpressible joy," because I trust in my God that I have never seen, and I have accepted his Son, Jesus, whom I have never met in the flesh. What about you? Notice that I said in the flesh, because I have met Him in the spirit. Ever since I met Him, my life hasn't been the same. The "inexpressible joy" that I have, the peace of mind that He gives me and the reward that I will receive once I meet Him in person are well worth the risk of serving a God whom I have never seen. Besides, when you are right, what is the risk? There isn't one!

God bless!

"Pray for the favor of God."

God's Favor

Scripture: *"For it brings favor if, because of conscience toward God, someone endures grief from suffering unjustly. For what credit is there if you endure when you sin and are beaten? But when you do good and suffer, if you endure, it brings favor with God."*

(I Peter 2:19-20 HCSB)

DEVOTIONAL

I have heard many Christians, including myself, pray for the favor of God. Until reading I Peter 2:19-20 I never realized that "enduring grief from suffering unjustly" is actually a way of gaining God's favor. I had been guilty of associating "suffering" with being under attack, and in some instances, my suffering *has* been part of an attack. However, if we suffer for God and the kingdom's sake, then we are not only (possibly) under attack, but we are also gaining the favor of God. To endure suffering in cases such as these means that God is pleased with us for not giving in or giving up in the face of adversity. That is a good thing! On the other hand, if we endure suffering because of a sin or when we are guilty of transgressing God's law, then our enduring is not a way of gaining God's favor but the just due for the sin or the wrong that we committed. It's like the scripture says, "happy are those who are persecuted for righteousness sake." We can rejoice when we are persecuted or we have to suffer. The key, however, is to make sure that we are not suffering because we have gone against the will of God.

God bless!

"We need to guard ourselves
from what we say about others
and how we treat others."

Happy Days

Scripture: *For the Scriptures say, "If you want to enjoy life and see many happy days, keep your tongue from speaking evil and your lips from telling lies. Turn away from evil and do good. Search for peace, and work to maintain it. The eyes of the Lord watch over those who do right, and his ears are open to their prayers. But the Lord turns his face against those who do evil."*

(I Peter 3:10-12 NLT)

DEVOTIONAL

If I had to give a title to the above scriptures, it would be "the key to enjoying life and having many happy days." Peter gives us the key to having a joyous life and experiencing happy days. Are you interested? I am and I'd like to share it with you! He says, "Keep your tongue from speaking evil and your lips from telling lies." Wow, isn't that interesting? He didn't say that the key to enjoying life or experiencing happy days is having a lot of money, fame, or prestige? No, the key to having what we all want (to enjoy life and to have happiness) is to be sure that our tongue speaks the truth and not evil. That means that we need to guard ourselves from what we say about others and how we treat others. We can't expect to have happiness or to enjoy life when we slander, backstab, talk evil about, or demoralize others, regardless of what they have done to us.

We must always take the high ground and do the right things: "search for peace, and work to maintain it." If you are having problems doing this, then think about this: "The eyes of the Lord watch over those who do right, and his ears are open to their prayers." You see, my friends, you have a vested interest in abstaining from evil. God is watching you.

Now, if that doesn't convince you to "keep your tongue from speaking evil and your lips from telling lies," then think about this. If you don't, God's ears are not open to your prayers and "He turns his face against those who do evil." On the other hand, if you do "keep your tongue from speaking evil and your lips from telling lies," then "his ears are open to your prayers" and "his face is turned toward you." Now, be honest, which one do you really want? Do you want God's ears to be opened to your prayers and for Him to be looking in your direction? Or do you want God's ears to be closed to your prayers and for Him to be looking away from you? I don't know about you, but I don't need to think about this one. I know what my answer is. I want God's ears to be open to me at all times and I want Him looking toward me and looking out for me every day of my life! I hope and pray that you want the same!

God bless!

All Power

Scripture: *"Now that He has gone into heaven, He is at God's right hand, with angels, authorities, and powers subjected to Him."*

(I Peter 3:22 HSCB)

DEVOTIONAL

This verse makes me think about my boss, the Commanding General, 2nd Marines Aircraft Wing. Under his command, he has some pretty powerful stuff at his disposal to assist a combatant commander with winning a battle or war. He can choose among fighter planes or jets, fighter helicopters or Cobras, heavy lift aircraft and other aircraft that do some pretty unique things that I can't mention. In other words, he is "the man," and "the man" can dispatch any of his assets when needed to assist others in fighting an effective campaign against the enemy.

Like the Commanding General, but on a much larger and more powerful scale, our elder brother (Jesus) has some pretty powerful stuff at His disposal to assist us with our fight against the enemy. First, He has the privilege of sitting next to God the Father, who has given Him "all power in heaven and on earth." This means that there is no other power greater than Jesus' power. Secondly, He has angels at his disposal and He can dispatch any of his angels when He wants to, anytime He wants to, and as often as He wants to. Lastly, all authorities and powers are subjected to Him, meaning that there is no power on earth, in heaven, beneath the earth or anywhere else that is not subjected to our elder brother, Jesus. Let me ask you one question. With a big brother who has this much horsepower at his disposal, what do we have to worry about when we have to do battle? You got it. Nothing! We don't have anything to worry about because our big brother is "the man," and He has everything that we need at his disposal just to assist us in winning any and every battle.

Stop worrying about anything. Your big brother Jesus can handle it, and He is in heaven at the right hand of God watching over you daily!

God bless!

Backsliders

Scripture: *"For it would have been better for them not to have known the way of righteousness than, after knowing it, to turn back from the holy commandment delivered to them. It has happened to them according to the true proverb: 'A dog returns to its own vomit,' and, 'a sow, after washing itself, wallows in the mud.'"*

(II Peter 2:21-22 HCSB)

DEVOTIONAL

Peter uses a pretty gruesome picture to describe what it is like for a Christian who has come into the knowledge of Christ and then returns to his/her old ways. Paul uses an image of "a dog returning to its own vomit." Just thinking about eating vomit makes me sick in the stomach, even as I type this "Thought for the Day." Well, just as this image makes me sick (and probably you, too), I am sure that when God shows us the error of our ways, and He sets us free from the error of our ways, and then we return to the error of our ways, he, too (God), gets sick in the stomach.

In fact, God gave John a similar image during John's banishment to the island of Patmos when the Lord spoke about "lukewarm" Christians. He said, "Because you are lukewarm, and neither hot nor cold, I am going to vomit you out of My mouth." Not a pretty picture, is it? You got it. It's not. For God to talk about our ways making Him so sick that He gets sick to the stomach to the point that He vomits, is not a pretty picture that I like to imagine. Neither do I want to be guilty of being like a "dog returning to its own vomit" or "a sow, after washing itself, wallowing in the mud." What about you? Well, here is how you and I can make sure that we don't make God sick to the stomach. Do not return to our old ways once God has delivered us, or once we have come into the knowledge of Him.

God bless!

Last Days

Scripture: *"Dear friends, don't let this one thing escape you: with the Lord one day is like a thousand years, and a thousand years like one day. The Lord does not delay His promise, as some understand delay, but is patient with you, not wanting any to perish, but all to come to repentance."*

(2 Peter 3: 8-9 HCSB)

DEVOTIONAL

I have never been one who paid much attention to predictions of when the Lord will return or when the world will end. I have always felt (and still do) that we should try to live each day as if it were our last day, and that each day should be lived for the glory of God. Many have asked me questions such as "Are we living in the last days?" or "Do you think the world is going to end soon?" I usually answer both questions with "I don't know," but from what I understand in scripture, we just may be living in the last days.

However, what the last days mean to us may not mean the same to God. As Peter reminds us, "don't let this one thing escape you; with the Lord one day is like a thousand years, and a thousand years like one day." The bottom line is this, I don't know when the world will end and neither does anyone else. We can make predictions, but why bother making predictions if we live every day as if it is our last day on earth and we live it for Jesus?

If we live each day like that, then whenever the last day is (or comes), we will be ready for it and be ready for Jesus' return. The last point that Peter makes in today's thought is this: "The Lord does not delay

His promise, as some understand delay, but is patient with you, not wanting any to perish, but all to come to repentance." Once again, how we understand one thing does not mean that this is how God understands it. But there is one thing certain and that is this: the Lord is patient with you and me and everyone else for one reason, and that reason is that He does "not want any to perish, but all to come to repentance." God will come when God is ready to return, and you and I need to make sure that we are ready whenever He decides.

God bless!

Fellowship

Scripture: *"If we say, 'We have fellowship with Him,' and walk in darkness, we are lying and are not practicing the truth. But if we walk in the light as He Himself is in the light, we have fellowship with one another, and the blood of Jesus His Son cleanses us from all sin."*

(I John 1:6-7 HCSB)

DEVOTIONAL

Say it ain't so! Sorry, I know that I shouldn't say "ain't" but I couldn't resist (smile). Why? It is interesting to see that John connects "fellowship with one another" to "walking in the light as He Himself is in the light." Could it be that John is saying that if you and I do not have "fellowship with one another," that you and I are not walking in the light but walking in "darkness?" That is exactly what he is saying. John is saying that if we want to walk in the light as Jesus walks in the light, then we must have fellowship with one another. Otherwise, we are walking in "darkness."

Some will ask, "What about those who do not want to fellowship with me?" Good question. To have fellowship does not mean to be buddy, buddy, or to be best friends. To have fellowship means that I love you with the love of Jesus regardless of how you feel about me. It means that I will speak to you regardless of whether or not you speak to me. It means to be at peace with you regardless of whether or not you want to be at peace with me. It means that I am willing to ask for forgiveness when I have wronged you and to forgive you when you have wronged me. You see, my friends, you don't have control over whether or not someone loves, respects, cares about, or fellowships with you, but you do have control over your own actions. You can't stop me from being in fellowship with you. You may stop speaking to me and you may stop loving me. You may stop associating with me, but you can't stop me from fellowshipping with you.

The fellowship that John is talking about is unconditional, and I don't need you to agree with me, speak to me, like me, or associate with me in order for it to be done. Therefore, I can make sure that I am walking in the light by making sure that I am in fellowship with you. Remember this, John tells us that "God is light, and there is absolutely no darkness in Him," and if we say "we have fellowship with Him, and walk in darkness, we are lying and not practicing the truth." If God is in me (and in you) and we have accepted Christ, then we should not want to be in darkness. Therefore, we must be in fellowship with one another. Period!

God bless!

Forgiveness

Scripture: *"If we confess our sins, He is faithful and righteous to forgive us our sins, and to cleanse us from all unrighteousness. If we say, 'We have not sinned,' we make Him a liar, and His word is not in us. My little children, I am writing you these things so that you may not sin. But if anyone does sin, we have an advocate with the Father-Jesus Christ the righteous One."*

(I John 1:9-10; 2:1 NASB)

DEVOTIONAL

I have met so many people who are gripped by their past and present sins, enslaved by their past and present guilt, and depressed because they have allowed themselves to fall for Satan's lie that they are not and have not been forgiven. In some cases, I have counseled some people who refused to believe that they had been forgiven and instead thought they didn't deserve forgiveness. If this is you or you are in this mind-set, I want to speak directly to you. Don't believe Satan's lie any longer! From this point forward allow God to set you free (today) by hearing what He said through John, "If we confess our sins, He is faithful and righteous to forgive us our sins, and to cleanse us from all unrighteousness." You see, my friends, when God forgives, He also cleanses. To be cleansed means that you and I are no longer guilty of the sin that we committed and therefore, we don't have to feel guilty. Feeling guilty will prevent you from receiving what Jesus died for: *your forgiveness.*

He paid the penalty for our sins and therefore we can do what John recommended, "confess our sins." John is clear that all of us have sinned.

I know there are some holy folks who walk around like they haven't sinned, but believe me, they have. In fact, John says, "If we say, 'We have not sinned,' we make Him a liar, and His word is not in us." Let me ask you this one question. Who is telling the truth, you or Jesus? John said that if you (or I) say that we have not sinned then we make Him (Jesus) a liar and his word is not in us. Now, I can't speak for you, but I know for myself that Jesus is not a liar because I know that I have sinned, and I hate to tell you this, but so have you, too. Just admit it, stop playing games with yourself (and God), and "confess." You will feel much better and you will experience the "cleansing" power of a righteous Christ. Praise the Lord for the last part of verse 1, "But if anyone does sin, we have an advocate with the Father—Jesus Christ the righteous One." When we confess, God forgives, and when God forgives, why should you try to undo his forgiveness for yourself or anyone else?

God bless!

INDEX OF DEVOTIONALS

Y

Z

CPSIA information can be obtained at www.ICGtesting.com
Printed in the USA
LVOW10s1212220414

382720LV00001B/1/P